BVLGARI

DANIELA MASCETTI   AMANDA TRIOSSI

BVLGARI

Abbeville Press Publishers
New York London Paris

Editor
Stefano Peccatori

Art director
FG Confalonieri

Editorial co-ordination
Tiziana Quirico

Technical co-ordination
Gianni Gardel

First published in the United States
of America in 1996 by Abbeville Press,
488 Madison Avenue, New York, N.Y. 10022

ISBN 0-7892-0202-6
© 1996 Arnoldo Mondadori Editore spa

English translation
© 1996 Arnoldo Mondadori Editore spa

All rights reserved under international copyright
conventions. No part of this book may be reproduced
or utilized in any form or by any means, electronic or
mechanical, including photocopying, recording, or by
any information storage and retrieval system, without
permission in writing from the publisher. Inquiries
should be addressed to Abbeville Publishing Group.

Printed and bound in Italy.

First edition

When the idea of publishing a book dedicated entirely to Bulgari was first mentioned, we were afraid that digging into the past to find our roots would have infringed a fundamental rule we have always tried to follow: to look ahead, to think of the future and to innovate, revolutionise and modernise. Nevertheless, further reflection led us to admit that, despite everything, after over more than a hundred years of history, the moment had arrived to go in search of these roots for, perhaps, they are directly correlated to our present.

Today this book exists, and it is with joy and pride that we leaf through its pages, pausing at anecdotes and events which, in print, have become like the mosaic of our history. With the same enthusiasm, we look at the images that bear witness to the evolution of our style, the same one which, over the years, our grandfather, parents and we ourselves have made, make and will continue to make in order to create, keep alive and improve our company.

This is why we would like to thank those who wanted to question us, who overcame our initial reluctance and revealed some of our little secrets, analysing so successfully not only our history, but also our creations and their artistic evolution.

If we may be allowed, we would like to dedicate this work to our father, Giorgio, but also to all those who have worked and are presently working with love and passion in this company. Finally, to our children in the hope that they will want to continue this activity which has been our life.

Paolo and Nicola Bulgari

Contents

The History of Bvlgari	9
The Evolution of the Bvlgari Style	45
The Use of Coins	111
The Power of Bvlgari Design	135
The Tubogas	151
A Unique Sense of Volume	159
Colour and Fabulous Gemstones	169
From the Idea to the Finished Object	193
Silver and Precious Objects	203
Watches	215
Perfumes	233
Bvlgari's Image	239

The History of Bvlgari

The Origins of the Family

The origins of the Bulgari family are to be found in a small Greek village situated in the Pindhos mountain range in Epirus, not far from the Albanian border. This is a region rich in historical and mythical traditions, cited by ancient poets and historians such as Homer and Thucydides. It is the land of the river Acheron – entrance to Hades – and of the famous sanctuary of Dodona, sacred to Zeus.

The family's early history – they were then known as Boulgaris (Βουλγαρης) – and their presence in the village of Kallarrytes (Καλλαρυτες) date back to the early part of 19th century. These facts are recorded in a document written by Costantino Bulgari on the basis of his father's memories (entitled *Memorie di Famiglia Raccontate dalla Viva Voce del Papà Sotirio dal* [sic] *Figlio Costantino e qui Appresso Trascritte con la Maggiore Fedeltà e Precisione Possibile*). Kallarrytes' economy was based largely on stock farming. However, it also counted among its inhabitants skilled metalworkers whose craft had been handed down by father to son since Byzantine times. In particular, the silversmiths of Kallarrytes were famous throughout Epirus for their production – reminiscent in style of Byzantine artefacts – of belts, buckles, buttons, earrings, sword sheaths and cartridge belts worked in debased silver.

The Bulgari ancestors were among the silversmiths of Kallarrytes. There is little information on Constantinos and his son Georgis (1823-1889). The latter, a skilled silversmith, used to travel Albania and Epirus to sell his crafts. On one such trip he met and married Eleni Strougaris (b. 1833) at Paramythia where he settled, opening a small shop. They had eleven children but only one survived: Sotirios (Σωτηρις), born on 18 March 1857, the founder of the Bulgari firm.

1. *Advertisement, 1970s.*

3. *View of Kallarrytes, the small Greek village situated in the Pindhos mountain range in Epirus, south-east of the capital Ioannina, and not far from the Albanian border. It was here that the ancestors of the Bulgari family lived and worked as silversmiths in the first half of the 19th century.*

2. Map of Greece, Archipelago and Part of Anadoli, *by L.S. de la Rochette, London 1791.*

Sotirios, a lively, proud and ambitious boy, spent his youth in Paramythia. Little is known of his childhood, though it was apparently a happy one; of those early days he recalled an excessive love for cakes and sweet syrups which often got him into trouble with his mother. In addition, he never forgot his first unpleasant and frightening experience: while returning home with a friend from a fair in a neighbouring village using a shortcut in the mountains, he was suddenly confronted by two bandits who robbed him of everything – including his clothes.

Epirus was then under Ottoman rule; Sotirios recalls how, around 1873, the Turks and Christians agreed to burn down Paramythia in order to rebuild it *ex novo*. In the ensuing blaze, the Boulgaris' shop was destroyed. Georgis and Sotirios, the latter by then a trained silversmith himself, left the village and started to work for Albanian beys – local rulers – especially for those who lived in the vicinity of Argyrokastro. Father and son never settled in one place, spending at most one month in a location before moving on to the next. Sotirios never forgot the bitterly cold winters of the Albanian mountains or those unsafe areas where he required the protection of Turkish gendarmes – *zaptie* – while transporting precious silverware. In 1876, while carrying some of his silver, Sotirios was the victim of an attempted robbery. This particular experience, and in general a feeling of constant precariousness, led the Boulgaris to consider the idea of expatriating. The decision was finally taken the following year, largely as a consequence of the outbreak of the conflict between the Russians and the Turks in the Balkans. During this war the insurrection of the Christians against the Ottomans in the Paramythia area was repressed with extreme brutality. The horrors of these events, coupled with the collapse in the silver trade caused by such hostilities, were instrumental in prompting the Boulgaris to leave their country. Sotirios never forgot what his father told him when the decision was taken: "Let's go, my son, let's leave this country where life has become impossible, and let us find a land where we can live and work in peace."

Towards the end of 1877 Georgis Boulgaris, having left his wife with her relatives, set off with Sotirios for Corfu. Here they settled. In the

4. *Portrait photograph of Sotirio Bulgari, the founder of the dynasty of Bulgari jewellers, taken in Rome, circa 1900.*

5. *Sotirio Bulgari photographed around 1910.*

spring of 1878 they opened a small workshop on the ground floor of a house in the San Rocco quarter. In due course they integrated into the Epirote community of Corfu and were joined by Eleni. Some of the artefacts produced by Georgis and Sotirios in those years – necklaces, bracelets, buckles and belts – survive in the Bulgari family's collection.

In spite of the relatively comfortable life which Corfu provided, the young, talented and ambitious Sotirios found it restricting and began to entertain the thought of moving on. The occasion arose when, by chance, he met an old acquaintance, Demetrios Kremos, a Macedonian silversmith who remembered Sotirios' skills in chasing silver. Kremos, who was en route to Italy, persuaded young Sotirios to join him. In the autumn of 1880, they sailed for Brindisi and then proceeded to Naples. There they opened a small shop in Piazza dei Martiri, where they sold their artefacts in silver and plate. One evening, while the two partners were dining, the shop was broken into and many of their products stolen. This unfortunate event prompted Boulgaris and Kremos to abandon Naples and leave for Rome, where they arrived on 18 February, 1881. All Sotirios had left in his pocket was 80 cents of a lira.

Life was hard at the beginning. Nevertheless, they managed to produce and sell small silver objects from a stall in front of the French Academy on the Pincio. The selling lasted only three days, as they were caught without a licence and stopped from trading. This short period, however, was quite profitable as the two partners had managed to make two hundred lira. Their lives picked up when a Greek sponge merchant, a certain Kindinis, offered to let the two partners display their wares in a corner of the window of his shop. This outlet was situated at the beginning of Via Sistina, the present location of the Hassler Hotel. Their wares – buckles, buttons, etc.– sold well and soon the two partners were able to open their own shop at 75 Via Sistina. Here their business flourished; their goods were sought after by a foreign clientele in particular. This success also led to the first disagreements between the two partners. The enterprising Sotirios parted, setting up his own shop in the spring of 1884 at 85 Via Sistina.

As business in Rome during the summer months was very quiet, Sotirios sought to capitalise on trade at summer resorts: he packed his limited stock and set off to find a suitable location. He settled for St Moritz, which even at that time was a fashionable mountain resort, where he concluded the summer season very satisfactorily. This success, however, was based on hard work: Sotirios woke up every morning at 5 to begin fusing and casting his silver, which he then chased until late at night in the workshop which doubled as his home. In 1888 he agreed to an arranged marriage with Eleni (later known as Elena) Basios (1870-1940), the seventeen-year-old daughter of Sotirios' parents' neighbours in Corfu. After their wedding in Corfu, the couple settled at 109 Via Sistina, where a year later their first son, Costantino Giorgio (1889-1973), was born. Their second son, Giorgio Leonida (1890-1966), was followed by three daughters – Maria

7. *Front of the first Bulgari shop at 28 Via dei Condotti, circa 1900. The shop front is inscribed: "S. Bulgari - Argenteria Artistica, Antiquités, Curiosités, Bijoux". The window displays are a good indication of the variety of goods which Sotirio was trading at the time. These ranged from silver, antiques and bric-a-brac to jewels.*

6. *Page from a catalogue, advertising Bulgari subsidiaries (circa 1910).*

8. *Front of the Bulgari shop at 10 b-c Via dei Condotti, circa 1905. The English name "Old Curiosity Shop", taken from the title of a Charles Dickens' novel, shows Sotirio Bulgari's aim to capitalise on aristocratic, wealthy British and American tourists. Sotirio Bulgari and Alessi Giannopoulos, one of the many Greek compatriots summoned by Sotirio to Rome, stand proudly on the threshold.*

9. *Front of the Bulgari shop at 10 b-c. Via dei Condotti in the 1920s. In comparison with the previous window displays, this shows the increased emphasis on fine jewellery. The latter in fact began to dominate the business during these years.*

Athena (1891-1976), Sophia (1893-1908), Alexandra (1895-1984) – and a third son, Spiridione (1897-1932).

As business thrived, Sotirios summoned his fellow countrymen and relatives to join him in Rome to help him cope with his increased work load. In 1894 he opened another shop in Rome at 28 Via dei Condotti. This shop front, as may be seen from contemporary photographs, was inscribed: "S. Bulgari – Argenteria Artistica, Antiquités, Curiosités, Bijoux". The inscription confirms that by this date Sotirios, known in Rome as Sotirio, had also italianized his surname Boulgaris. The shop front, furthermore, gives an idea of what Sotirio was trading at the time: a variety of goods ranging from silver, antiques and bric-a-brac to jewels.

During these years other subsidiaries were opened: San Remo (1895), Naples (1897), Bellagio (1897) and Sorrento. Sotirio's successful summer seasons in St Moritz prompted the opening of "Saison d'été" premises at Pontresina in the Engadine and at Lucerne, in addition to his two outlets in St Moritz-Bad. By 1905, Sotirio had managed to secure larger and more prestigious premises at no. 10 b-c Via dei Condotti, on the ground floor of Palazzo Lepri. The inscription on the front of this shop indicates Sotirio's ongoing activity abroad. Furthermore, the store's English name, "Old Curiosity Shop", taken from the title of Charles Dickens' novel, shows that his aim was to capitalise on aristocratic, wealthy British and American tourists. It was during these years that he began to widen his stock to include an increased selection of jewels and items of personal adornment. Although Sotirio was clearly very proud of his numerous subsidiaries, he soon realised the necessity of concentrating on one location in order to succeed and excel in the field of jewellery and silver. Gradually he began reducing his network, either by closing or by handing over his shops to relatives. For example, the Sorrento subsidiary was ceded in 1908 to his brother-in-law Giorgio Basios.

The first decade of the 20th century were the formative years for Sotirio's sons Costantino and Giorgio, to whom he taught the secrets of the trade. They gradually became involved in the running of the firm, mainly dealing with antique silver and jewellery. Shortly

10. *A family holiday photograph of Sotirio Bulgari and his wife Elena with their two sons Giorgio and Costantino. Varese, September 1932.*

11. *Posthumous portrait of Sotirio Bulgari painted in 1933 by Renato Tomassi. Sotirio is portrayed proudly holding a silver-gilt Ravensburg nuptial cup dating from the second half of the 16th century. This was a favourite piece in his fine collection of antique silver.*

thereafter, however, the First World War brought the business to an almost total standstill; nevertheless, from 1918 on it began to flourish again. By that point, their future had been decided: the Bulgari would become famous jewellers and would collect fine silver and objects of art to serve as a backdrop to their gems.

Sotirio died on 24 November 1932, leaving the business in the hands of his two sons. In spite of the economic crisis of the early 1930s, Costantino and Giorgio decided to expand. In 1933 the premises of 10 b-c Via dei Condotti were enlarged to include the adjacent no. 10a, and the revamping of the shop was entrusted to a team of architects. The plans were drawn up by Florestano Di Fausto; the details were the work of Antonio Mina and Eugenio Scanferla. The lavish marble work, which included an imposing façade of travertine and green African marble, as well as an interior fitted with marble

12. *Lavish interior and exterior of the Bulgari shop at 10 a-b-c Via dei Condotti after the renovation completed in 1934 as published in the Enciclopedia Treccani to illustrate the entry "negozio" (shop). The entrance hall, which remains unaltered to date, is decorated with gilding and marbles. The niches are adorned with the Crown of the German Emperor, the Crown of St Edward (England), the Royal Crown of Bohemia and the Royal Crown of Hungary, known as the Crown of St Stephen, which serve a purely decorative purpose.*

13. *A pair of Chinese carved spinach-green jade table screens, circa 1800, on contemporary hardwood stands. These objects were part of the Bulgari jade collection which included outstanding examples and was displayed in the* Galleria delle Giade *(Jade Gallery).*

columns and ancient Imperial Egyptian porphyry urns, was carried out by the Medici firm. Fine cabinets and lavish gilding completed the interior. This new shop, which was inaugurated on 9 April 1934, so fulfilled contemporary ideas of what a business outlet should look like that both its façades and its interior served to illustrate the entry "*negozio*" (shop) in the most important Italian encyclopaedia, *Enciclopedia Treccani*.

After the death of their father, the two brothers divided their responsibilities in the business; while different, their roles were nonetheless complementary.

Costantino was interested in objects of virtue, and built up the Bulgari collection of snuff boxes, icons, objects of art and jade carvings. His particular interest, in line with the family tradition, was silver. He purchased and collected fine antique examples of work by English,

14. Ubaldo Crescenzi, "Maestro Orafo" (Master Goldsmith), photographed at work in 1954. From 1925 to 1965 he managed the workshop which produced Bulgari jewels. His long-standing association as a business partner and loyal friend of the Bulgari family were instrumental to the success of the firm.

15. View of the Bulgari workshop in 1936, situated at this date above the shop at 10 Via dei Condotti.

16. *Portrait of Costantino Bulgari, by Carlo Romagnoli, 1938.*

German, French, Danish, Russian and Italian silversmiths. On a visit to Lisbon in 1930, Costantino, who considered himself an expert in antique silver, was surprised to discover a masterpiece of religious art commissioned by King John V of Portugal in 1743-1750 from Roman silversmiths. In particular he was struck by the beauty of a pair of large silver torch stands, the work of the Roman silversmith Giuseppe Gagliardi, whose name was completely unknown to him. This incident spurred him to devote himself to the study of Italian goldsmiths, silversmiths and gem engravers, which led to the compilation of the first comprehensive directory of all Italian silver masters, both famous and not so famous, accompanied by their registered marks. He began his research in the archives of the Roman goldsmiths guild at Sant'Eligio and was able to make good progress during the Second World War, when business once again came

17. *A view of the* Sala degli Argenti *(Silver Gallery) of the Bulgari shop in Rome reserved for the display of fine, rare and antique silver objects.*

18. *Silver sculpture of* Ulysses and Argos *by Stefano Fedeli (Rome, 1815-1866). Originally purchased by Costantino Bulgari who particularly appreciated the work of Roman silversmiths. The group portrays Ulysses on his return to Ithaca, after twenty years of adventures and tribulations, as he is reunited with his old and faithful dog Argos. This object is now part of the permanent collection of the firm. Examples of Roman silver of the late 18th and early 19th century included in the Bulgari collection and illustrated in these pages are evidence of the high quality and refinement of their design and craftsmanship. These objects rival in beauty and finesse the best examples of contemporary French and English silver.*

19. *Silver sculpture of* Patroclus and Menelaus *by Vincenzo II Belli (Rome, 1815-1859). The group depicts Menelaus, the King of Sparta, lifting from the ground Patroclus who had been killed by Hector during the Trojan war. Belli was master silversmith between 1828 and 1859 and "Console dell'Arte" from 1835 to 1843.*

practically to a standstill. After 1945, when the firm began to thrive again, Costantino was unable to dedicate enough time to his research. The project was held up until his brother Giorgio, recognising how much it meant to him, assumed full responsibility for the day-to-day running of the business and allowed Costantino to devote time to his research. Years later, Costantino acknowledged his brother's generosity by dedicating his *Argentieri, Gemmari e Orafi d'Italia* to his brother: "I'm grateful to my brother Giorgio for having given the most important – if indirect – help, by taking on more responsibility in managing our company, thus allowing me the time required for

20. *A gold, polychrome enamel and pearl ring set with a grossular garnet (hessonite) cameo of a cherub, attributed to Giacomo Anfossi (b. 1505), second half of the 16th century. The back of the bezel is inscribed:* "GREG XIII". *Anfossi, a well-known goldsmith of his time began working for the Papal Court in Rome in 1548, and was at the service of Pope Gregory XIII Boncompagni from 1573.*

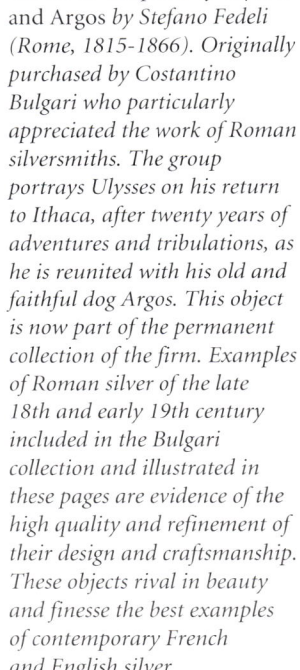

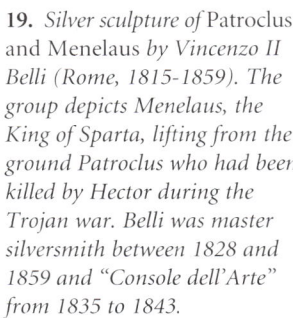

THE HISTORY OF BVLGARI

this book." Published between 1958 and 1974, in five volumes, this major work is the only existing directory of Italian silver hallmarks from all periods. The knowledge and experience acquired in the preparation of such a large-scale work of scholarship unquestionably brought Costantino to the forefront of dealers and connoisseurs in this field. Although now overshadowed by the international success which Bulgari has achieved with jewellery and watches, antique silver – in particular pieces made by Roman masters such as Valadier, remains one of the firm's renowned areas of expertise.

If Costantino may be regarded as the scholar, Giorgio undoubtedly should be seen as the businessman. Ever since the beginning of his involvement in the firm, he concerned himself with the creative aspect of the business, using his expert knowledge of stones, jewellery design and manufacture. At the age of 18 he travelled to Paris, then – as it had been since the Middle Ages – the creative centre for jewellery design. There he began buying precious gemstones and was exposed to the fashionable trends in jewellery, an experience which proved to be fundamental for the future development of the firm. The survival of his "Passeport de Première Classe" (ill. 24) issued by the Greek Consulate General in Rome in 1913, which allowed him these frequent trips abroad, describes him as a tall, blond man with blue

21. Silver soup tureen (Rome, 1787-89), by Giuseppe Valadier. Giuseppe (b. 1762) was the son of Luigi Valadier, one of the greatest Roman silversmiths of the 18th century. He learned his skills in his father's workshop and later turned to architecture. Amongst his major achievements in this field is the project for Piazza del Popolo and the Pincio in Rome. This tureen is probably part of a set of four designed to symbolise the four seasons. The finial designed as a child wrapped in a cape warming his hands next to a burner, suggests that this is an image of Winter.

22. A fine and rare pair of Neo-classical silver candlesticks (Rome, 1792), by Vincenzo Coaci (b. 1756), master silversmith from 1783 to 1794.

21

eyes and regular features. Interestingly, this document also confirms that, in 1913, the Bulgari still retained their Greek nationality.

Giorgio's kindness extended to everybody. His old friend and colleague, the gem dealer Charles Manfred Newton, recalled – in *A Barrel of Diamonds* (1980) – not only his good taste, knowledge, foresight and shrewdness but also his warmth of heart. A witty conversationalist, Giorgio's talk was spiced with aphorisms such as "*Bambini e quattrini mai troppi*" (you can never have enough children and money) or "*Se son rose fioriranno*" (if they are roses, they will blossom). His death in 1966 was a sad loss for his family, his employees, his friends and the jewellery world at large. Obituaries mourned him and praised his outstanding qualities: "G. Bulgari, the jeweller of Kings died [...] his display of jewels in Via Condotti were famous throughout the world [...] the public considered the lavish

23. *Posthumous portrait of Giorgio Bulgari by Renato Tomassi, 1966.*

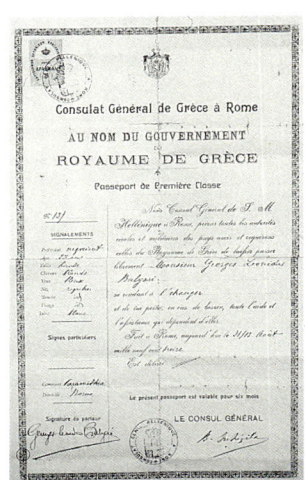

24. *"Passeport de Première Classe" issued to Giorgio Bulgari by the Greek Consulate General in Rome in 1913. This document allowed him to travel frequently to Paris, then the centre for jewellery design. Here he was exposed to the fashionable trends in jewellery. This experience proved to be fundamental for the future development of the firm.*

25. *A view of the shop-front taken in the late 1950s showing an elegant display of important jewels and silver. The shop-windows and entrance are framed by green African (*verde Africano*) marble cornices which stand out against the backdrop of sandy-beige travertine. Travertine, in Latin* lapis tiburtinuus, *quarried near Rome, was a stone favoured in buildings in ancient Rome and was used for example in the Coliseum. The marbles used in the lavish decorations of the shop were fashioned from fragments of ancient Roman ruins.*

26. *View of the interior of 10 Via dei Condotti in the 1960s showing the lavish decor of the* Galleria delle Giade *(Jade Gallery) embellished with ancient Imperial Egyptian porphyry urns and* verde Africano *and* Antico di Grecia *marble columns.*

27. *A portrait photograph of Laura Gulienetti, Costantino Bulgari's wife, taken in the 1920s. She is wearing long pearl and diamond earrings typical of the firm's production of those years.*

shop situated opposite the Caffè Greco as a mythical attraction in front of which one could dream and let one's imagination run..." (*Paese Sera*, Rome, 8 March 1966).

During the war Costantino and Giorgio Bulgari had helped both members of the Roman Jewish community and Allied troops. As a sign of gratitude they were awarded certificates by the British Supreme Allied Commander, Field-Marshal H.R. Alexander, and Commanding General J.T. McNarney of the United States Army in the Mediterranean for their help, "which enabled them [the Allied troops] to escape from, or evade capture by the enemy."

29. *A group portrait of Costantino's family painted by Renato Tomassi in 1933 during a summer holiday in Arcinazzo near Fiuggi. From left to right: Costantino's wife Laura and daughters Marina, Xenia and Anna.*

30. *Giorgio Bulgari and his wife Leonilde photographed whilst on holiday in the Swiss Alps near St Moritz, 1932.*

28. *Sotirio, Giorgio and Leonilde Bulgari photographed at the Lido of Venice in 1932.*

31. *Giorgio Bulgari with his niece Anna, in the early years of her involvement with the firm. Rome, 1948.*

The third generation of Bulgari – Costantino's daughters Anna (b. 1927) and Marina (b. 1930), and Giorgio's sons Giovanni, known as Gianni (b. 1935), Paolo (b. 1937) and Nicola (b. 1941), and daughter Lia (b. 1933) – had also been brought up to carry on the family tradition. It was in 1965, partly as a consequence of Giorgio's illness, that his three sons took over the management of the business.

Anna Bulgari Calissoni worked by her father's side helping him with the purchase of silver objects. She was also involved in the design of jewels and silver until 1984 and remained a silver consultant for the firm until 1990. After Costantino's death she inherited her father's legacy and continued to research the field of Italian silversmiths. In 1987 she published *Maestri Argentieri, Gemmari e Orafi di Roma*, an invaluable survey on Roman silversmiths; this will be completed with a further work on the subject.

Marina Bulgari Spaccarelli was involved in numerous aspects of the business ranging from administrative tasks to design, and she kept a prominent position in the firm until 1976.

From childhood Gianni showed a particular inclination towards design, which became his field of expertise within the firm. He was also responsible for buying gemstones, using his good eye and expert knowledge. A handsome man, he was considered in the 1960s one of the most eligible bachelors and his sightings with glamorous women of the day were frequently the subject of speculation in newspaper gossip columns. In 1975 he was kidnapped and held captive for one month. This incident attracted national and international media coverage and the name Bulgari became headline news. His association with the firm ended in 1987.

Paolo, the current Chairman of the firm, keeps a low profile, out of the reach of publicity; yet his quiet façade belies the depth of his creative talents which have been developed by the experience of years of work alongside his father. In the creative process, he endeavours to pass on his family legacy by working in close collaboration with a team of trusted and skilled designers and craftsmen. He is widely acknowledged as one of the world's foremost jewellers, in terms of both technical skills and inspiration.

33. *Paolo Bulgari, Chairman, Nicola Bulgari, Vice Chairman, and Francesco Trapani, Chief Executive Officer. Rome, 1995.*

32. *The three brothers Gianni, Paolo and Nicola Bulgari photographed in the shop in Rome, 1980.*

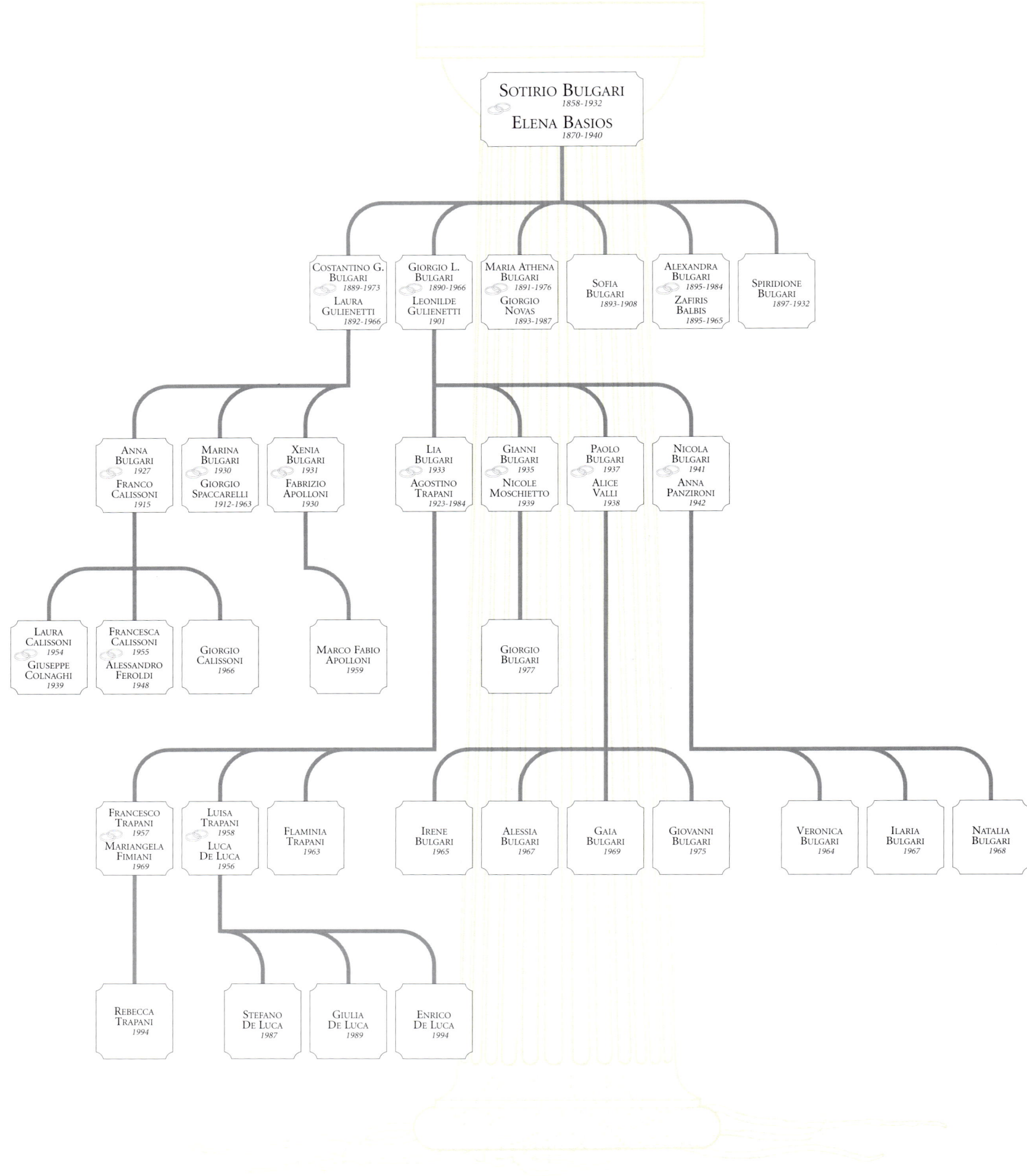

34. *Bulgari's family tree.*

Nicola, now Vice Chairman, since 1970 shares his time between Rome and New York. He continues to pursue his interest in silver, keeping alive the firm's tradition. He has always been fascinated with history, and since childhood he has collected ancient coins. This early passion led to the extensive use of coins in Bulgari jewellery. He is an outgoing and ebullient person, a born salesman. He still remembers how as a boy he spent days in the shop "nosing around, using my ears and my eyes and trying to make myself useful." As a young man, he extended his knowledge – initially acquired by working next to his father and uncle – by training as a diamond cutter in Amsterdam.

Clearly, the two Bulgari brothers now in charge – Nicola and Paolo – are as different in personality as the two brothers of the preceding generation.

Veronica (b. 1964), Nicola's daughter, joined the firm after studying art history at the Courtauld Institute of Art in London, and in 1995 became United States Assistant Area Manager for the firm's recently launched luxury perfumes.

Irene (b. 1965), Paolo's daughter, is based in Paris where she assists the Avenue Montaigne operation with public-relations work.

Since 1981, Francesco Trapani (b. 1957), son of Lia Bulgari, sister of Paolo and Nicola, has joined his uncles in running the firm. After graduating with honours from the University of Naples, his studies were completed with courses in business administration at New York University. These qualifications enabled him in 1984 to take up successfully the position of Chief Executive Officer of the firm. From this position he has managed the company's international growth and diversification, which have transformed Bulgari into one of the world's most promising groups in the luxury goods market.

In the summer of 1995 he oversaw an initial public offer of approximately 36% of Bulgari shares on the Italian Stock Exchange and on London's SEAQ International. The aim of this capital infusion is to enable the company to expand and diversify in the luxury goods market, responding to its enduring prestige and success.

Chairman Paolo Bulgari stated (*The Times*, London, 5 May 1995) that while the long term objective is to become an international luxury goods holding company, "Bulgari's success shows how, in certain conditions, there are no contradictions between growth and the preservation of one's own culture."

Bulgari and Its Patrons

Since its beginning, the firm's success relied on a wide national and international clientele which included industrialists, royalty, aristocrats, politicians, heads of State, businessmen, artists, and also creative people – stars of stage and screen. An indication of the passion with which Bulgari jewels have always been collected is given by records of certain Roman princesses trading their land in exchange for Bulgari jewels.

In the years preceding the Second World War, among the most regular patrons of Bulgari was Count Vittorio Cini of Venice, who purchased, among countless other objects of art and jewels, an exceptionally fine fancy pink diamond of 24.44 carats.

Purchase records which span from January 1936 to May 1943 document the regular acquisition of jewels and objects of art on behalf of the dapper diplomat Count Galeazzo Ciano di Cortellazzo, Minister for Foreign Affairs in Italy from 1936 to 1943. Ciano,

35. *Clare Boothe Luce, the glamorous American Ambassador to Rome, photographed in 1963 wearing a fine emerald and diamond necklace by Bulgari, illustrated on page 75.*

36. *Tyrone Power and Linda Christian choosing their wedding rings assisted by Ubaldo Crescenzi. Rome, 1952.*

37. *Sophia Loren wearing a Bulgari necklace and earrings photographed with Jane Mansfield in the early 1960s.*

together with his wife Edda, Mussolini's daughter, purchased goods worth a total of 300,000 lira, a phenomenal amount of money for the time and circumstances. Among their purchases, which range from diamond-set bracelets, gold bracelets, pocket watches, clips and gold cigarette cases, one finds an entry on 17 June 1939 for a gold lining for a metal wedding band. This suggests that Count Ciano, who had given up his gold wedding band for the country following requirements dictated by the international sanctions imposed in 1935, could not tolerate this base metal band and commissioned Bulgari to disguise in it a gold lining. These documents indicate also the glamorous lifestyle led by the couple, considered at the time the third most important family in Italy after Mussolini and the Royal Family. Indeed, Edda played the role of Italy's first lady until the year before her husband's execution in 1944, by order of Mussolini, on the accusation of treason.

Since the 1920s, the success of Bulgari was also made by a prolific American patronage which included industrialists such as copper magnate William Boyd Thompson. Thompson was known to dock his magnificent yacht in the port of Civitavecchia and then head immediately to Bulgari in Rome. In the following decades Bulgari, with its world-wide reputation, was a point of reference for wealthy Americans such as Barbara Hutton, Florence Gould, Henry Ford II and Nelson Rockefeller. Samuel Henry Kress, American businessman and founder of a chain of "Five and Ten Shops", had a standing account at Bulgari between 1930 and 1940 for his beautiful companion, Mrs Kilvert. Her sumptuous Bulgari parures became legendary in New York.

The glamorous United States ambassador to Italy, Clare Boothe Luce, was also an admirer of Bulgari. She was appointed by President Eisenhower in 1953, the first woman to be an American envoy to a major country. Extremely successful in her post, she was affectionately dubbed by the Italians "*la Luce americana*" (the American Light). In a 1963 photograph she is seen wearing an exceptionally fine emerald and diamond necklace by Bulgari, purchased during her stay in Rome (ill. 35). Throughout her life she continued to patronise Bulgari and even as an octogenarian she owned a gold, hematite and diamond

38. *Elizabeth Taylor photographed in front of Bulgari's at 10 Via dei Condotti, 1967.*

39. *H.M. the Queen Mother of the Hellenes, H.M. Queen Anne Marie of the Hellenes, H.R.H. Princess Irene of Greece and Denmark and H.R.H. the Princess of Spain, née Princess Sophia of Greece and Denmark (later Queen of Spain) strolling in front of Bulgari, 1974.*

40. *The 1970s top model Veruschka in front of Bulgari, 1970.*

41. *Merle Oberon accompanied by Bruno Pagliai in 1963. The actress is wearing a Bulgari flower-spray brooch, a typical creation of the time.*

parure typical of the firm's production in the 1980's. Also jewellery lover Evita Peron is known to have visited Bulgari in Rome. For this reason Bulgari created a replica of the floral diamond brooch of the 1950s, illustrated on page 76, which will be worn by Madonna in Alan Parker's film *Evita* of 1996.

In her autobiography, *Footprint* (1980), Brooke Astor recalls how on a visit to the Connaught Hotel in London in 1958, her invalid husband Vincent "amused himself by having old Mr Bulgari [Giorgio] come over from Rome to discuss an emerald necklace and earrings for me. Mr Bulgari, a sophisticated and worldly old man, stayed for lunch in our sitting room. He promised to assemble some stones and send his designs. Vincent was very pleased with himself and said, 'Even though your old man is laid up he has done a fine bit of work for Pookie.'" Two years later, after his death, when Mrs Astor was trying to adjust to life without him came the news, via a coloured transparency, that the parure was ready. She wrote: "I did not feel in the mood to buy myself such an expensive present, but I went to see my banker and he said: 'Vincent ordered it for you and wanted you to have it. If you like it yourself I think you should buy it.' I did like it. Vincent liked jewellery and had very good taste. It is pretty and not ostentatious but very elegant, so I bought it. Considering it was

42. *Italian actress Virna Lisi passing in front of Bulgari, 1971.*

43. *Kirk Douglas photographed in front of Bulgari, 1964.*

44. *Klaus and Ruth Kinski with their young daughter Nastassia walking in front of Bulgari, 1965.*

45. *Audrey Hepburn with her son Sean entering Bulgari, 1973.*

47. *Actress Claudia Cardinale photographed for* Vogue Italy *in 1993 wearing four Bulgari gem-set bracelets.*

48. *Sophia Loren photographed for* Vogue Italy *in 1993 wearing a spectacular diamond demi parure from the Bulgari Collection Internationale created in 1992. The necklace and earrings are respectively set with 152.78 carats and 15.11 carats of diamonds.*

46. *Susan Sarandon wearing a Bulgari necklace photographed with Tim Robbins in 1993 on the occasion of the 65th Annual Academy Awards in Los Angeles.*

49. *Bill Gates, Chairman of Microsoft, photographed in 1995 wearing a* BVLGARI-BVLGARI *wristwatch.*

Vincent's last personal gift to me I am very sentimental about it." It is interesting to note that this necklace was remarkably similar to the one owned by Clare Boothe Luce.

Since the 1920s Hollywood stars such as Mary Pickford, Kay Frances, Gary Cooper, Shelley Winters, Tyrone Power, Zsa Zsa Gabor and Grace Kelly, later Princess Grace of Monaco, have either bought or owned Bulgari jewels. Countless celebrities have regularly visited the Bulgari shop in Rome from the years of the *dolce vita* on: Audrey Hepburn, Mel Ferrer, Gina Lollobrigida, Sophia Loren, Ingrid Bergman, Lee Radziwill, Virna Lisi, Merle Oberon, Ursula Andress, Kirk Douglas, Anna Magnani, Romy Schneider, Laura Antonelli, Charles Bronson, Jill Ireland, Mireille Darc, Veruschka, Klaus Kinski, John Wayne, Tony Curtis, Alice and Helen Kessler and Mina are immortalised in front of the Bulgari shop in Rome.

At the time of her marriage to the writer Erich Maria Remarque in 1958, Paulette Goddard, who was renowned for her passion for fine jewels, also purchased from Bulgari. She favoured ornaments set with rubies and diamonds in particular.

For Richard Burton, who gave Elizabeth Taylor a Bulgari ring during the filming of *Cleopatra* in 1963, visiting Bulgari premises was a new and exciting experience. "I introduced her to beer," he is known to have said, "and she introduced me to Bulgari." If for Burton Bulgari was a novelty in 1963, for Liz it had become customary to receive Bulgari jewels. During those turbulent days of *Cleopatra*, she was conflicted over her relationship with Burton. Her fourth husband, Eddie Fisher, made the last attempt to save their marriage: he rushed out to Bulgari and bought her a fabulous emerald necklace. Life with Elizabeth had taught him the therapeutic value of such gifts; he knew that a beautiful jewel would make everything wonderful for some time.

The American artist Andy Warhol, obsessed with design, colour, shape and texture – all so essential to his own aesthetics – also admired and collected jewels by Bulgari. He said that each time he visited Rome he called at Bulgari, "because it is the best exhibition of contemporary art." He liked the gold chains set with ancient Greek and Roman coins, such as the gold necklace of filed curb linking set with a Roman bronze *centenionalis* of Constantius II (AD 337-361) sold as part of his estate in 1988.

Film directors and producers such as Carlo Ponti and Roberto Rossellini have shopped at Bulgari for Sophia Loren and for Ingrid Bergman, their respective wives. Vittorio De Sica is known to have been a client since 1939.

50. *Sophia Loren with Marcello Mastroianni in Robert Altman's film* Prêt-à-Porter *(1994). The actress is wearing the ruby and diamond necklace illustrated on page 172 with a pair of matching earrings.*

51. *Paolo Bulgari with Claudia Schiffer and her fiancé David Copperfield seen at the launch of the* Chandra *collection in Paris, 1994, recorded in the film* Prêt-à-Porter. *The supermodel is wearing a* Chandra *heart-shaped pendant.*

52. *Isabella Rossellini wearing Bulgari jewels, with Nicola Bulgari and his daughter Veronica, at "Tribute to Nature" charity event, New York, 1991.*

53. *Paolo Bulgari and Sharon Stone at the presentation of the* Chandra *collection in Athens, 1994. If on this occasion the actress wears only one necklace, in Martin Scorsese's film* Casino *of 1995 she is showered with millions of dollars of Bulgari jewels.*

54. *Bulgari jewels have frequently been featured on the front covers of glossy magazines worldwide.*

Bulgari's association with the film industry has been strengthened in the last decades. In the 1970s American actress Jessica Lange was frequently seen wearing Bulgari jewels; for example, she wore panelled gold, emerald and diamond earrings in a photograph on the April 1979 cover of the American magazine *Interview*. Her seven-year exclusive contract with Dino de Laurentiis also included an association with Bulgari. In her first film, *King Kong* (1976), Lange – although scantily dressed and for most of the time in the clutches of the monster – still had the opportunity to show off Bulgari jewels for which the firm still receives credit.

More recently, the *Quadrato* watch was featured on the wrist of Glenn Close in the film *The Paper* (1994). A Bulgari steel and gold *Parentesi* necklace features as the first prize of a lottery in the film *Il Conte Max* (1991) starring Christian De Sica and Ornella Muti.

In his 1994 film, *Prêt-à-Porter,* starring Sophia Loren and Marcello Mastroianni, director Robert Altman included a scene depicting the launch of the *Chandra* collection at Bulgari in Paris. In this scene Paolo Bulgari plays himself and Sophia Loren flaunts a magnificent Bulgari ruby and diamond necklace and earrings (ill. 50, 197). Claudia Schiffer was wearing jewels from the *Chandra* collection: a heart-shaped pendant, three gem-set bracelets and a ring (ill. 51).

Since the 1990s the firm has frequently loaned jewels to film stars to be worn on important occasions such as the Academy Awards; to Glenn Close in 1993, for example, and to Susan Sarandon in 1994. Bulgari also gave a BVLGARI-BVLGARI watch to Anthony Hopkins in honour of his Oscar for *The Silence of the Lambs* in 1991.

Monarchs and members of Royal Families from all over the world, from Greece to Denmark, from Belgium to Britain, from Spain to Persia, from Thailand to Saudi Arabia and Egypt, have visited Bulgari in Rome throughout the years and admired and purchased their creations. In keeping with Bulgari's traditional discretion and confidentiality, these names are never disclosed, with the exception of those who agreed to be the Guests of Honour at charity events sponsored by Bulgari.

55. *H.R.H. The Duchess of York, H.R.H. The Duke of York and Nicola Bulgari, Venice, 1990.*
H.R.H. Princess Alexandra of Kent, Paolo Bulgari, Nicola and Anna Bulgari, Versailles, 1991.
H.I.H. Prince Akishino of Japan and Paolo Bulgari, Tokyo, 1991.
H.R.H. The Duke of Edinburgh with Nicola and Anna Bulgari, Waldhurst Park, Great Britain, 1991.
H.M. King Juan Carlos I of Spain with Paolo Bulgari and Francesco Trapani, Madrid, 1991.
H.R.H. The Princess Royal and Nicola Bulgari, London, 1995.
H.M. Queen Sirikit of Thailand and Paolo Bulgari, Bangkok, 1992.

The Evolution of the Bvlgari Style

Early Days

When Sotirio set up his business in 1881-1882 in Rome, he chose Via Sistina right in the fashionable centre of the newly appointed capital. This road was also where the contemporary novel by Gabriele d'Annunzio, *Il Piacere*, unfolds; the opening scene describes the elegant and decadent hero Andrea Sperelli waiting for his lover Elena in Palazzo Zuccari in Via Sistina.

Sotirio's shop at no. 85 was crowded with silver artefacts probably in large part created by him. These wares included chased silver salvers, spoons, goblets and vinaigrettes; among the stock there were also silver items of personal adornment and jewellery such as buckles, girdles, chains and chatelaines. Unfortunately, besides a few surviving objects of the early days in Rome (ill. 58-61), there are no existing written records of the goods traded by Sotirio during those years.

However, photographs of the window displays of Sotirio's shop at 28 Via dei Condotti (ill. 7), opened in 1894, confirm that the wares he sold were very similar to the few examples now in the family's private collection.

In addition, the shop front inscribed "S. Bulgari - Argenteria Artistica, Antiquités, Curiosités, Bijoux" is a further indication of the variety of the stock, with the emphasis on ornamental silver as opposed to utilitarian flatware. The fact that part of the inscription was in French, then the fashionable international language, denotes an undeniable degree of sophistication. The goods that one could purchase at Bulgari at the time, however, were the middle range of precious objects traded in Rome at the turn of the century.

Sotirio's success enabled him to move by 1905 to larger and more prestigious premises. The new shop at no. 10 Via Condotti (ill. 8) had a large window display flanked by glass fronted cases, all on marble

56. *Advertisement, 1965-67.*

bases. Once again evidence of the stock is provided only by contemporary photographs of the shop's display. These are full of important silver ware prominently exhibited, such as large and richly embossed trays, ladles, spoons and mirrors. In addition there is a range of ceramic wares: figurines, plates and vases possibly from the renowned Capodimonte factory. Jewellery by now occupies a large portion of the display, which is carefully and tastefully arranged. Gold longchains set with gemstones are draped on the shelves, while necklaces, earrings and pendants are displayed on stands, and suspended gold mesh evening bags complete the arrangement.

From what one can deduce from these images, it appears that Bulgari after 1905 was still trading items reminiscent of 19th-century tradition which did not in any way reflect current trends dictated by Parisian jewellers. This is not surprising given that Rome in those days was culturally and artistically stagnant. For example, in terms of jewellery design, the Art Nouveau movement which originated in France in the 1890's and swept across Europe from Spain to Scandinavia never deeply affected Italy. It certainly never reached

57. *A group of silver ornaments manufactured by Georgis Boulgaris, Sotirio's father, all chased with elaborate decorations reminiscent of Byzantine taste. The earliest surviving object, a silver bracelet decorated with lion masks, dates to the early 1870s when Georgis was still working in the Epirote town of Paramithya. The elaborately chased buckle, the girdle formed of twelve oval medallions, possibly depicting allegorical figures of War and Peace, and the vinaigrette were produced from about 1875 to 1885, the years which coincide with Georgis' activity in Corfu. Besides silver artefacts Georgis also produced in Corfu base metal ornaments such as the bracelet set with faux coins of the seven Aegean islands.*

THE EVOLUTION OF THE BVLGARI STYLE

47

58. *A group of chased and pierced silver ornaments manufactured by Sotirio for his first shop in Rome at 85 Via Sistina between 1884 and 1905. It was during these years that Sotirio worked relentlessly: his day would begin at 5 a.m. by fusing his silver. He then worked on the chasing of his objects until late at night. Amongst the earliest objects are a buckle and two chatelaines, one with an oval medallion possibly depicting Hebe produced between 1884 and 1895. It is interesting to note that a number of items are stamped with Sotirio's maker's mark, at times simply "s.b.," or with his monogram, or even with both marks accompanied by no. "800," the standard for silver.*

Rome, which continued to be steeped in the archaeological revival style of 19th-century tradition. It is interesting to note that the only concession to the "modern" style is the ironwork consisting of sinuous foliate scroll-work which frames the sign "S. Bulgari". The fact that other branches – "Napoli, Lucerne, St Moritz-Bad" – are listed on the façade is a clear indication of Sotirio's success and expansion (ill. 8). By 1894 Sotirio had two shops in Rome, one in Naples at 42 Via Calabritto, and two seasonal outlets in St Moritz and Lucerne, described at the time as "*succursales d'été*". It is also interesting to note how Sotirio by now had abandoned the French inscription used above his 28 Via dei Condotti shop in favour of the English of "The Old Curiosity Shop". This clearly shows that he was addressing a new, affluent, British and American clientele.

Around 1908 Giorgio Bulgari, Sotirio's son, began travelling abroad. His favourite destination was Paris, which since the Middle Ages had been the creative centre for jewellery design. It was here that he observed the many variations of the then fashionable Garland style mastered by Cartier. This style of jewellery was largely inspired by decorative elements found in Louis XVI art, such as garlands of floral and foliate motifs, wreaths and fluttering ribbon bows, rendered in platinum and mainly set with diamonds and pearls. In Paris Giorgio was not only exposed to new jewellery design but also to new manufacturing processes such as working with platinum. It was

59. *Details of Sotirio's maker's mark struck on his artefacts at the end of the 19th century showing his initials "s.b." and his "sb" monogram. The two marks seem to be used indiscriminately and at times both are found on the same object.*

THE EVOLUTION OF THE BVLGARI STYLE

60. *A silver spectacle chatelaine pierced and chased in an elaborate floral and foliate pattern. It was produced between 1892 and 1898 for Sotirio's shop at 85 Via Sistina probably by Nessis, one of the Greek compatriots summoned to Rome by Sotirio in the late 19th century.*

THE EVOLUTION OF THE BVLGARI STYLE

indeed only around 1900 that platinum began to be used extensively for jewellery in France. This precious white metal had not been used before on a large scale, mainly because of the difficulty of working it, due to its melting point, which is much higher than any other metal then used in jewellery. The use of platinum offered the advantages of white pieces, which were at once structurally very sound and yet delicate and lacy in appearance: platinum is, unlike silver, an untarnishable white metal of great strength.

The only surviving example of Bulgari jewellery in the Garland style is a design for a platinum and diamond bracelet consisting of a succession of eight light and delicate oval links connected by fluttering bow motifs (ill. 63). This scanty evidence for production in the first decades of the century is not surprising, as the firm's archives of this early period are themselves very scarce. Furthermore it is likely that Bulgari, like other jewellers of the time, until the late 1920s did not sign its creations, making attribution difficult.

61. *Other silver items which were produced by Sotirio at a slightly later date (1895-1905): a girdle pierced in a foliate scroll design and three chased and pierced buckles, two depicting mythological scenes.*

62. *A chased and embossed 19th-century silver presentation-dish. Its decoration was probably inspired by an earlier French Renaissance example. It is interesting to note that this dish features prominently in the window displays of the "Old Curiosity Shop" in about 1905 and has remained a treasured possession of the Bulgari family.*

51

63. *A rare design in the Bulgari archives for a platinum and diamond bracelet (circa 1905) in the fashionable Parisian Garland style. It shows how the firm by this date was producing fine jewels in line with international trends.*

The 1920s

By the 1920s the success of the firm and its new emphasis on jewellery rather than silver can be substantiated by contemporary photographic records of the shop front of 10 b-c Via dei Condotti. In the large window three important diamond necklaces tower above a display of smaller jewels exhibited in their elegant cases with hinged sides (ill. 9). In this instance the linear and geometric design of the necklaces is not outmoded but to the contrary reflects the fashionable style dictated by Parisian jewellers of the day. The fact that the silver is exhibited in the lateral windows confirms that by this date the firm had shifted its attention to jewellery. The displays are no longer crowded as in the former "Old Curiosity Shop". By now quality and not quantity was important – very precious gem-encrusted necklaces and rare examples of antique silver vases and cups are displayed elegantly

64. *A selection of ten designs for earrings of the mid-1920s: some dated 1924 clearly illustrate the current trends of Art Déco design. All earrings are characterised by linear and geometric shapes, strong contrasting colours and stylised decorative motifs often derived from exotic sources. The stylised lotus motif of Egyptian inspiration as well as carved Chinese jade are very typical decorative elements for the time.*

THE EVOLUTION OF THE BVLGARI STYLE

53

spaced. The fact that the inscription "S. Bulgari" towers above the shop front is an indication that the firm was by now very well established and renowned and that the name Bulgari was sufficient to attract clientele.

As mentioned, jewels sold by Bulgari during the 1920s reflected in all aspects the fashionable trends of the time. In 1925 the "Exposition Internationale des Arts Décoratifs et Industriels Modernes" in Paris promoted innovative jewels in the style thereafter known as Art Déco, from the abbreviation of the name of the exhibition. These "modern" jewels were based on linear designs, stylised naturalistic decorative elements and gemstones of contrasting colours. Among the most fashionable items of jewellery were long sautoirs and earrings of very pronounced vertical and geometrical design, like those worn by Laura Gulienetti Bulgari in a contemporary portrait photograph (ill. 27). These jewels combined precious gemstones such as emeralds, rubies, sapphires and diamonds in daring chromatic juxtapositions with semiprecious stones such as coral, jade, onyx, rock crystal, turquoise and lapis lazuli. All such features are clearly visible in Bulgari's designs for pendant earrings of 1924 (ill. 64, 65).

The decorative motifs of Art Déco jewels were characterised by great eclecticism and ranged from pure geometric shapes to stylisation of

65. *Three designs for pendant earrings of the 1920s.*

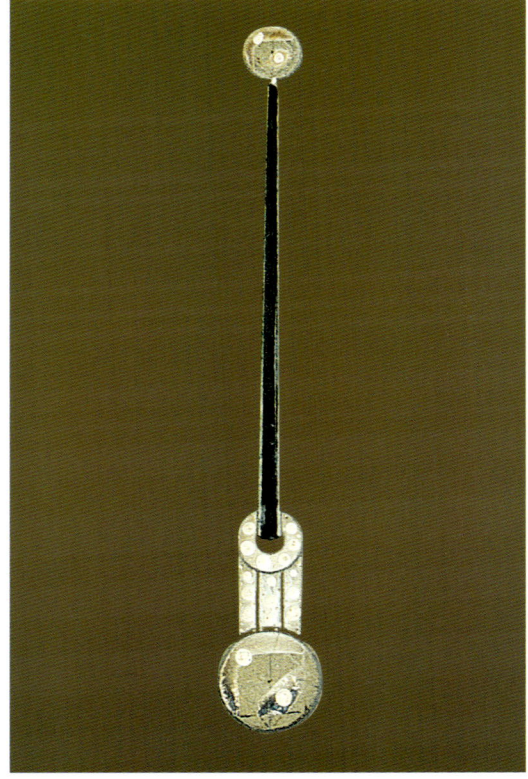

THE EVOLUTION OF THE BVLGARI STYLE

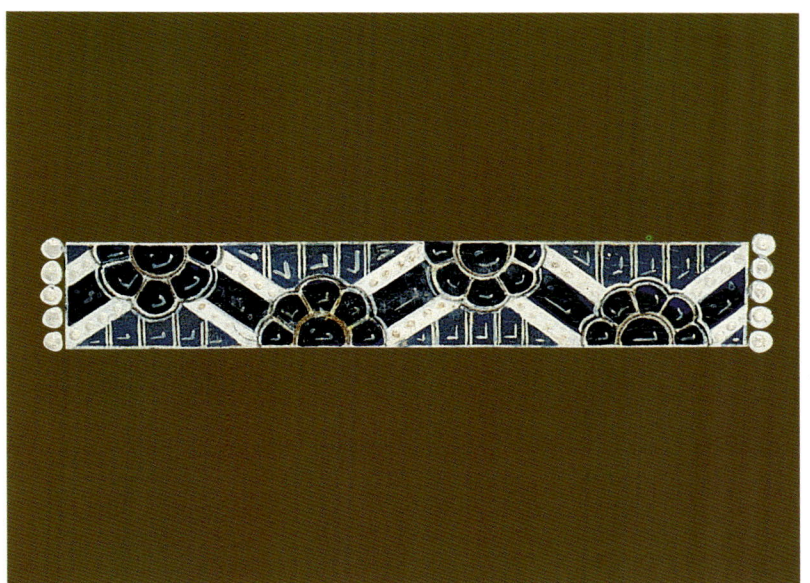

66. *These designs for brooches of the mid-1920s illustrate the typical use of domed calibré-cut coloured gems, often employed for stylised floral motifs.*

67. *Two designs for wristwatches, 1920s.*

68. *A platinum, onyx, black enamel and diamond lapel watch of the 1920s. Characteristically, the case is decorated with pavé-set diamonds juxtaposed with black onyx. The dial is signed "BULGARI", in line with the firm logo at the time, with a "U" rather than a "V".*

nature, from a reinterpretation of elements deriving from exotic Oriental cultures to ancient Egyptian art. The latter in particular came to fashion following the sensational discovery of the treasure of Tutankhamun in 1922. The stylised lotus flower – the main decorative element in the designs for two earrings by Bulgari – is clearly part of this particular trend (ill. 64). A good example of Oriental inspiration is provided by two jade earrings (ill. 64) set with Chinese carvings. The typical use of domed calibré-cut coloured gemstones utilized for the rendering of stylised floral motifs is visible in the designs for brooches and wristwatches (ill. 66, 67).

Bulgari kept abreast of the development of jewellery design. Towards the end of the 1920s jewels tended to become heavier and more massive, a feature which one can readily recognise in Bulgari's designs of the time, often set with coloured cabochon stones.

1925 is the year that marks the beginning of a long-standing collaboration and friendship between the Bulgari family and Ubaldo

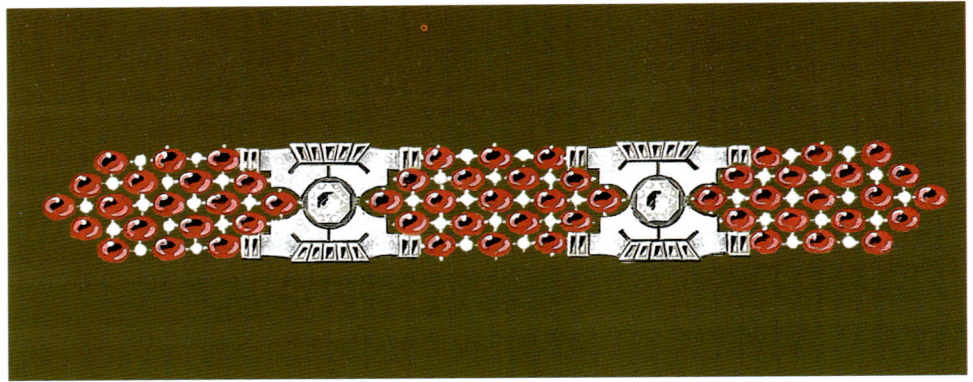

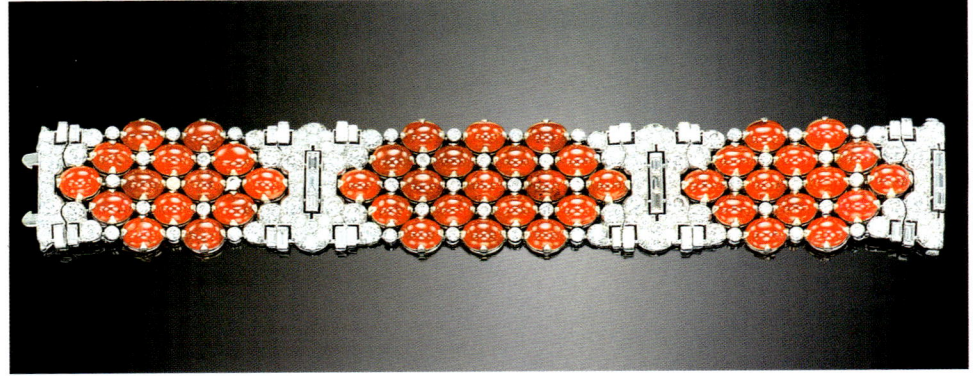

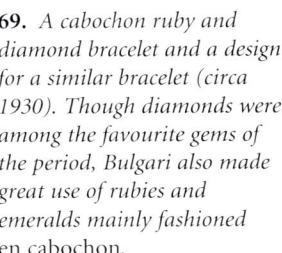

69. *A cabochon ruby and diamond bracelet and a design for a similar bracelet (circa 1930). Though diamonds were among the favourite gems of the period, Bulgari also made great use of rubies and emeralds mainly fashioned en cabochon.*

Crescenzi (1903-1965). From his workshop situated initially in Via della Fontanella di Borghese and later above the Bulgari shop at 10 Via dei Condotti (ill. 14, 15), Ubaldo translated into precious metal and gemstones designs conceived by Bulgari. Not all jewels at this time were designed and manufactured in Rome, however: there is evidence that Bulgari entrusted the design and manufacture of some jewels to various Parisian workshops. These jewels are recognisable by the fact that the French assay marks and maker's marks accompany the Bulgari signature.

70. *This platinum and diamond rose brooch of the late 1920s is a good example of the jewels which were manufactured in Paris for Bulgari.*

The 1930s

A jewellery exhibition held at the Palais Galliera in Paris in 1929 marked the beginning of a further development in jewellery design: coloured gemstones began to be displaced in favour of a monochromatic use of diamonds mounted in platinum. This trend was voiced by Georges Fouquet in his article in *L'Orfèvrerie, la Joaillerie* published in 1942, where he stated: "*Si la characteristique de l'Exposition de 1925 avait eté la 'couleur' celle de Galliera s'affairmait dans la note blanche.*"

Once again Bulgari was in tune with Parisian developments: the firm began creating jewels set entirely with diamonds, characterised by bold geometric shapes inspired by the machine age and by industrial design. The repetition of mechanical chains, bolt and nut motifs together with stylised buckles and straps formed the basis for most

71. *A rare example of a diamond tiara of 19th-century inspiration produced by Bulgari around 1930. The interior of its elegant case is surprisingly stamped:* "S. BULGARI. 10 VIA CONDOTTI, ROMA". *This suggests that the transformation of the logo from* "S. BULGARI" *to* "BVLGARI" *was a gradual process. It was probably initiated by Sotirio in the early 1930s, before his sons took over the firm.*

72. Three diamond bracelets dating to the late 1920s and early 1930s. In line with current fashion, they are all formed by a succession of geometric motifs set with diamonds of different cuts – brilliant, baguette, marquise and dart-shaped – mounted in different settings. It is interesting to note that they are all signed "BULGARI" with a "U".

jewels of this period. The play of colour typical of the 1920s was replaced by a play of light achieved by juxtaposing diamonds of different cuts in different settings, which reflected light in a variety of ways. These features are clearly visible in numerous designs and jewels by Bulgari produced at the time (ill. 72).

All the bracelets are in fact formed by a succession of geometric shapes and are decorated mainly with diamonds of different forms and cuts – brilliants, baguettes, trapezes and marquises – in various settings such as claw, collet or pavé. Brooches, double clips and even important necklaces conform to these parameters of design. In the 1930s it was particularly fashionable for women to adorn their lapels and necklines with clips, and to wear more than one diamond bracelet at a time. Bulgari capitalised on the fashion of the time producing a large number of bracelets and double clips. As can be seen from the

73. *Five designs for diamond-set bracelets of the 1930s. Characteristically, the bracelets are formed by a succession of geometric elements mainly set with diamonds. One bracelet is punctuated with three prominent sugar-loaf cabochon emeralds – a type of cut favoured by the firm in the following decades.*

74. *Nine designs for diamond and gem-set brooches and double clips of the 1930s. Characteristically, they are all of geometric design; some are embellished with large central coloured gems.*

75. *A fashionable diamond brooch (1935). It is typical for its strictly geometric design set entirely with diamonds.*

77. *A ruby and diamond Trombino ring of 1934, given by Ubaldo Crescenzi, head of the Bulgari workshop, to his future wife Pierina for their engagement.*

examples, bracelets were always formed by long bands of equal width; this feature enabled women to wear such bracelets one above the other and have them rattle on the wrist (ill. 69, 73).

In general Bulgari jewels of the 1930s conform to fashionable Parisian style both in design and in type; but the design for important necklaces stands apart. A motif that distinguishes Bulgari's necklaces of this period is the regular punctuation by circular elements of large brilliant-cut diamonds. This feature was not used to the same degree by other jewellery houses (ill. 79-82).

Another distinguishing characteristic of Bulgari at the time, in spite of the general monochromatic diamond trend, was the use of large coloured stones frequently placed in prominent positions; emeralds, rubies and sapphires both faceted and cut *en cabochon* can all be found. For example, a large cabochon ruby forms the centre of the

78. *Front and side view of a fine Trombino diamond ring, 1932. This type of ring was first created in the early 1930s and is one of the most successful and long-standing Bulgari designs. It consists of a wide pavé-set diamond shank which extends into a high bezel set with a large gem. The shoulders are always decorated with baguette diamonds placed horizontally. The illustrated example is remarkable not only because it is one of the very first the firm created but also because the diamonds are set on the entire hoop.*

76. *A fine brooch of the 1930s, set at the centre with a large step-cut emerald in a surround of baguette and brilliant-cut diamonds. In all its features it is typical of its time and is similar to the designs illustrated opposite.*

79. *A fine diamond-set necklace of the 1930s. Though most of Bulgari jewels of this period conform to the then fashionable Parisian style, the design for important necklaces stands apart. A distinguishing feature is the punctuation of the design with large brilliant-cut diamonds, an expedient which was not employed to the same degree by other jewellers.*

design of a geometric plaque brooch (ill. 74-76) and a substantial octagonal step-cut emerald is set at the centre of a diamond plaque brooch. In addition, the panels of the geometric bracelets are at times set with coloured stones such as the sugar-loaf cabochon emeralds in the bracelet illustrated (ill. 73).

Towards the end of the 1930s Bulgari designs, in common with those of other jewellers, were characterised by greater movement, no longer

constrained within symmetrical and strictly geometrical forms. A good example of this trend are the ruby and diamond flower brooches and the double clip formed of plaited ribbon motifs set with calibré-cut emeralds (ill. 83). Furthermore, the clip of sun-burst design, which also dates from this time, demonstrates with its use of yellow gold and honey coloured citrines how Bulgari is responding once again to novel and fashionable trends. Cartier, around 1937, also launched a new line of jewels set in yellow gold rather than platinum, decorated with citrines of burnt and golden hues.

One of the most successful and long-lasting designs by Bulgari, the *Trombino* ring, dates to the 1930s. Among the first examples was that given by Giorgio Bulgari to his future wife Leonilde on the occasion of their engagement in 1932 (ill. 78). This ring was called *Trombino* as its shape is somehow reminiscent of a small trumpet (*tromba* in

80. *Two diamond-set necklaces of the 1930s illustrating Bulgari distinctive design.*

THE EVOLUTION OF THE BVLGARI STYLE

81. *A diamond-set necklace of the 1930s, characteristically punctuated by the use of large brilliant-cut diamonds.*

82. *A fine diamond necklace convertible into a tiara of the 1950s. It is a good example of how Bulgari continued to punctuate the design of elegant diamond-set necklaces with large brilliant-cut stones, a feature the firm developed as early as the 1930s. Noticeably, this example is characterised by softer lines although the overall pattern and details such as the clasp are indebted to the 1930s.*

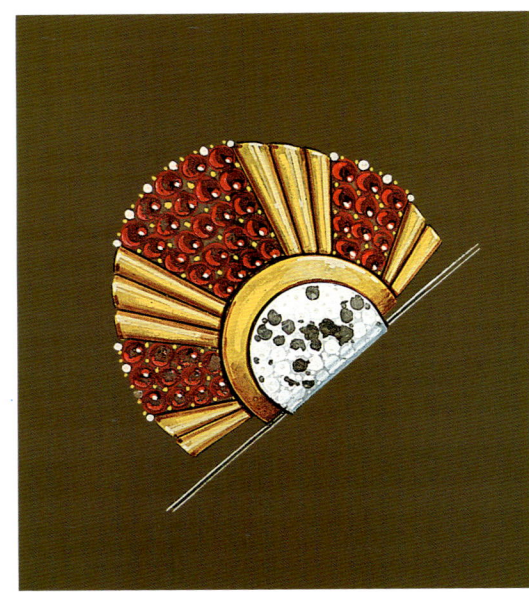

83. *Designs for brooches and double clips of the late 1930s illustrate the development of jewellery of the time. Naturalistic motifs such as flowers replaced in these years the earlier rigid and geometric designs. Gold and citrines were used instead of platinum and diamonds.*

Italian). It consists of a wide pavé-set diamond shank which extends into a high bezel set with a large stone, either a diamond or a coloured gem. The shoulders are typically decorated with a series of baguette diamonds placed horizontally and the bezel is given an extremely fine finishing touch of metal fretwork.

After Sotirio's death in 1932, and following the lavish refurbishing of the premises in via Condotti commissioned by Costantino and Giorgio between 1932 and 1934, the firm's name changed from "S. BULGARI" to "BVLGARI". The inscription on the shop front was modified and written in block capitals as found in Roman inscriptions (ill. 12). This stylish logo has never been changed since and is as striking today as it was when first devised. Existing examples of signed jewels of the time confirm that, at times, the Bulgari signature was engraved on pieces in this new style of inscription.

THE EVOLUTION OF THE BVLGARI STYLE

84. *Five designs for gold and gem-set bracelets of the 1940s.*

The 1940s

During the 1940s Bulgari was forced to considerably reduce the production of jewellery. The outbreak of the war caused the jewellery trade to come almost to a standstill throughout Europe. This was in part because the general climate was not conducive to lavish display of jewellery but also because of widespread legislation which aimed to control the industry. On 3 September 1941, just over one year after Italy's entry into the world conflict, legislation was passed forbidding the purchase and sale in Italy of all precious metals, pearls and gemstones and all artefacts which included such materials.

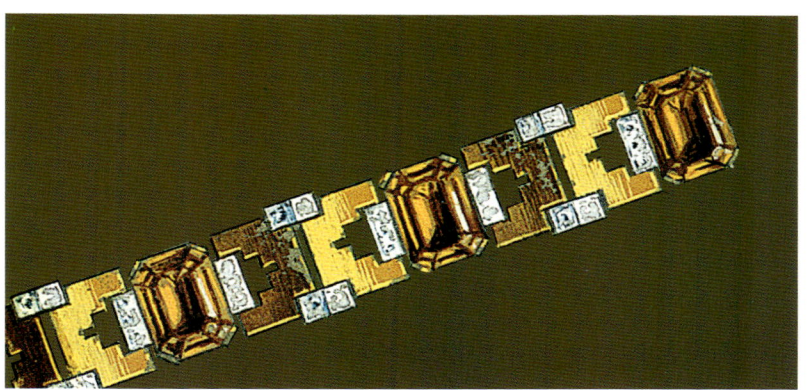 

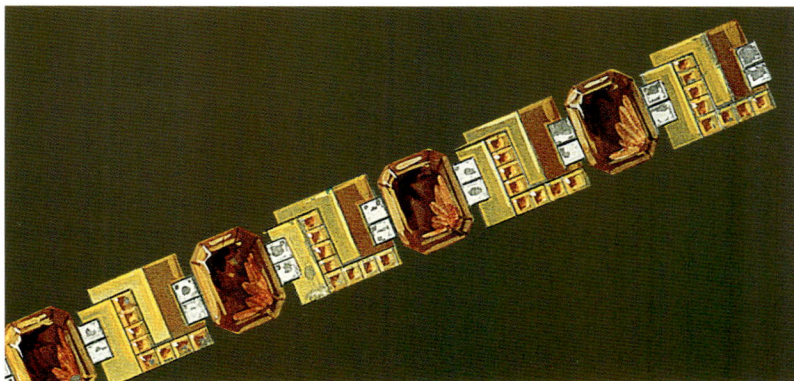 

85. Two bracelets, one formed by pink and yellow gold cone-shaped links, the other of furled yellow gold elements and two similar designs, all dating to the 1940s. These illustrate once again how Bulgari conformed to the fashionable trends of the day. By 1940, largely due to wartime restrictions, gold of different hues set either with very small precious gemstones such as rubies or with large semiprecious stones such as citrines had universally replaced platinum encrusted with diamonds.

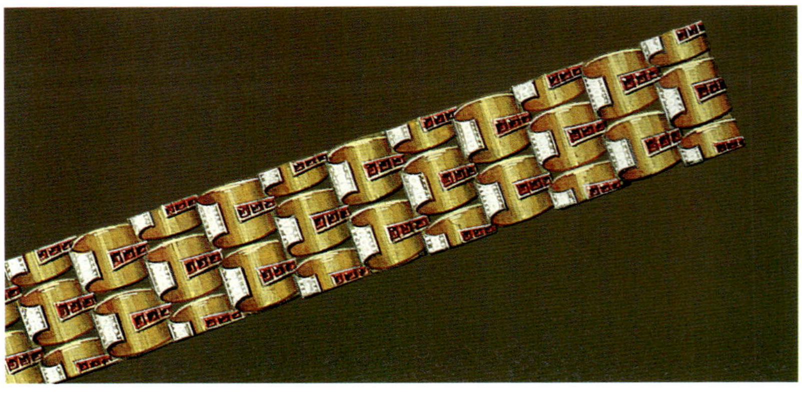

THE EVOLUTION OF THE BVLGARI STYLE

86. *Front and reverse of one of a pair of gold and diamond clips (circa 1940), typically set in yellow gold. The diamonds are old-cut, which suggests that the stones were unset from an earlier jewel – a common practice because of wartime restrictions on trading precious materials.*

On 21 October of the same year, an amendment to the earlier decree allowed the use of precious materials in connection with the arms industry. Only religious artefacts made of precious metal, silver watches, and gold wedding bands under 5 grams in weight were exempted from this restriction. In addition, the remodelling of jewels or the making of new ones was allowed only if all materials were supplied by the customer.

In spite of Bulgari's restricted production during the war years, the jewels that were manufactured once again followed trends of the day. By the 1940s the rigid geometric shapes typical of the 1930s were abandoned in favour of softer shapes often of naturalistic inspiration: gold of different hues frequently set with semiprecious stones such as citrines replaced platinum encrusted with diamonds. Gold clips, gold bracelets and designs by Bulgari clearly demonstrate this new trend of the 1940s (ill. 84-86).

These were also the years that saw the reintroduction of a flexible tubular chain constructed with no soldering, which had been employed extensively in jewellery of the 1860s and 1870s. In the 1940s this chain was renamed *Tubo gas*, due to its resemblance to the tube of a petrol pump or a gas hose. Since then it has remained an all time favourite for necklaces, bracelets and watches at Bulgari (ill. 175, 176).

87. *A pair of flowerhead cluster earclips, set respectively with yellow and blue sapphires, circa 1945. These jewels illustrate how still, during the 1940s, Bulgari was influenced to a great extent by the fashionable Parisian designs of the day.*

The 1950s and 1960s

The economic prosperity after the war prompted a comeback in the 1950s of high jewellery characterised by flowing designs lavishly set with diamonds and precious gemstones mounted in white metal. Unquestionably, diamonds reigned supreme during this decade, epitomised by the song *Diamonds are a Girl's Best Friend* sung by Marilyn Monroe in the 1953 film *Gentlemen Prefer Blondes*.

Asymmetrical knots and bows, favourite decorative motifs for brooches and necklaces, are well represented in Bulgari's production of the time. In particular they served as an ideal vehicle to offset rare and precious gemstones for which Bulgari was especially renowned during this period.

The particular feature of setting fine gemstones in unobtrusive mounts continued to be a characteristic of Bulgari in the following decade. In the early 1960s, in fact, thanks to designer Gianni Valli (1916-1991), who worked with the firm from 1945 until 1990, Bulgari rivalled the finest Parisian jewellers in creating asymmetrical floral sprays often mounted *en tremblant* (ill. 91, 93-96).

Since the 18th century, floral motifs interpreted in a realistic manner and arranged in freeform compositions had been a constant theme in French jewellery. The apogee of the flower jewel conceived in this fashion was perhaps reached in the mid 19th century by Parisian jeweller Oscar Massin (b. 1829) and it continued to flourish except during the Art Déco period, when flower motifs came to be stylised.

From the end of the 1950s, all areas of design in Italy began assuming a clearly recognisable identity which started to be internationally acclaimed. Therefore it is not surprising that in 1962 for the first time Italian jewellers exhibited their production in Paris, the world's shrine

THE EVOLUTION OF THE BVLGARI STYLE

88. *A fine necklace designed as a double festoon of step-cut diamonds and emeralds, early 1950s. Characterised by flowing lines and fluttering ribbons, this jewel is similar to the best Parisian designs of the day.*

89. *A fine necklace of the 1950s. The diamond florets support a fringe of nine pear-shaped Colombian emeralds weighing 25 carats total. The matching earrings are set with four pear-shaped emeralds for a total of 23.15 carats. The combination of one of the three precious coloured gemstones – emeralds, rubies, sapphires – with diamonds is another typical feature of all high jewellery of this period.*

90. *A fine necklace of the late 1950s, formerly the property of Clare Booth Luce, set in platinum with twenty-seven oval emeralds weighing a total of approximately 25.50 carats and baguette and brilliant-cut diamonds for a total of approximately 39.50 carats. It is representative of Bulgari's style of the time, especially its use of fine emeralds in surrounds of diamonds.*

91. *A colourless diamond flower spray brooch of 1957 is among the first of this series of jewels. A replica is worn by Madonna, in Alan Parker's film,* Evita *(1996).*

92. *A pair of earclips of 1961 formed by double flowerhead motifs set with a combination of sapphires and diamonds.*

THE EVOLUTION OF THE BVLGARI STYLE

93. *In the late 1950s Bulgari purchased an extraordinarily fine and large collection of naturally coloured diamonds of the most diverse colours and shapes. This prompted the creation of a series of flower spray brooches where diamonds – coloured and colourless – are set in unobtrusive mounts. The flowerheads are all mounted en tremblant: on spring settings which allow them to flicker at every movement. This very fine flower spray brooch of 1959 is set with one deep yellow and ten intense blue diamonds, in colourless diamond surrounds.*

for fine jewellery. In particular the exhibition of 1962 – "Bijoux italiens. Goût et tradition dans la joaillerie italienne" – was chosen to mark the opening of the Italian Institute in Paris. Seventy-five Italian jewellers exhibited a total of ten thousand jewels with the intent to show both tradition and modernity in Italian jewellery design.

In the same year an article in the English trade magazine *Watchmaker, Jeweller and Silversmith* extolled the qualities of Italian jewellery design and stated "Italy has built her post-war revival upon design. She has, in the space of a few years, come to be the design centre of Europe. Europe drives cars designed by Italians, buys Italian furniture, or furniture copied from Italian models, and Europe walks in Italian shoes; Europe, too, is currently buying Italian jewellery."

Bulgari, which until the 1960s had on the whole followed French design and the Parisian way of conceiving jewellery (ill. 88-91), from

94. *A flower spray brooch of 1958 set with six golden yellow diamonds of various cuts in a surround of colourless stones. This brooch may also be adapted to be worn as a hair ornament.*

95. *A flower spray brooch of 1960 decorated with diamonds of various hues, ranging from golden yellow to cognac colour, set in platinum.*

96. *Two flower spray brooches of 1962 (above) and 1960 (below), set respectively with variously shaped rubies, sapphires and diamonds. The reverse illustrates the* en tremblant *spring mechanism which allows the flowerheads to quiver.*

THE EVOLUTION OF THE BVLGARI STYLE

97. *A fine ruby and diamond necklace of 1961 designed as a garland of flowers. A typical early 1960s Bulgari creation in its floral design and emphasis on fine gemstones.*

98. *A flower spray brooch of 1961, set with sapphires and diamonds.*

then on also began to take distance from it and forge a new and distinct style. This was a gradual process; from the illustrated examples one can notice how Bulgari began to depart from flowery asymmetrical motifs, moving towards more structured, symmetrical and compact shapes.

It was also during these years that Bulgari began creating jewel sets with highly important gemstones enclosed in smooth rather than jagged borders. The frequent use of marquise-shaped stones all orientated in the same direction provided a rounded and smooth outline for these jewels. This was a feature which was in stark contrast with the design of most other high-quality jewellery of the day, which relied especially on spiky frames formed by alternating marquise, pear-shaped and circular stones.

This particular departure marked the beginning of one of the most constant elements in Bulgari design: that of creating jewels

99. *A flower spray brooch of 1962 set with fancy coloured diamonds of various shades of golden yellow and cognac.*

THE EVOLUTION OF THE BVLGARI STYLE

100. *A collection of jewels dating from 1956 to 1965 including a ruby, sapphire and diamond demi parure of stylised flowerhead cluster design (1956), and two other brooches. The annular one, created in 1961, is set with cabochon emeralds, rubies, sapphires and diamonds; the other, of 1962, is set with cabochon emeralds and sapphires, and diamonds.*

and artefacts characterised by very smooth and linear contours. It was during this period that Bulgari also began to create jewels marked by a sense of volume. This particular feature was obtained by using cabochon-cut coloured stones in prominent positions, and was an innovation as such stones had not been used in this manner during the 20th century.

In addition, Bulgari began exploring striking colour combinations. Different gemstones came to be chosen and combined not so much for their intrinsic value but for their chromatic effect. In this sense Bulgari was breaking away from the conventional restricting triad of emerald, ruby and sapphire which characterised most jewellery of the day (ill. 100, 101, 102, 104).

In other words Bulgari – by introducing jewels with smooth contours, with a sense of volume and interesting colour combinations – was laying the foundations for its future style. A decade or so later this would appear mature and more fully fledged.

To the eyes of contemporaries, however, these features were already distinctive and recognisable as the "Bulgari style." An article of

101. *A ring of the early 1960s, set with a cabochon sapphire in a surround of rubies and diamonds.*

THE EVOLUTION OF THE BVLGARI STYLE

102. *Two demi parures of 1969-70 of stylised flowerhead cluster design, one set with cabochon emeralds, rubies and sapphires, the other with cabochon amethysts, emeralds and sapphires, highlighted in both cases by diamonds.*

104. *A diamond and gem-set necklace (1962), formerly the property of Ingrid Bergman, designed as a chain of diamond scrollwork supporting eighteen large cabochon sapphires alternating with ruby clusters. The bold juxtaposition of colours – red, blue and white – not featured in the same way by other contemporary jewellers, was a peculiarity of most of Bulgari creations at this time. Interesting colour combinations were and continue to be one of the firm's main concerns.*

103. *A page of designs from a Bulgari sketch-book dating to the mid-1960s.*

BVLGARI

105. *A page of designs from a Bulgari sketch-book dating to the late 1960s - early 1970s. Note the predominance of cabochons and the vibrant colour combinations.*

December 1963 in *Connaissance des Arts* confirms the distinctive aspect of Bulgari jewels by stating: "*un bijou Bulgari se reconnaît comme se reconnaît un tailleur Chanel...*"

The 1960s also marked the beginning of the use of ancient coins mounted in jewellery. From this time on coins have remained a constant element in Bulgari's production. One of the earliest examples is a necklace of 1966 with two gold *solidi* of Justinian I (AD 527-565) and a *solidus* of Leo I (AD 457-473) mounted at the front (ill. 152). An antique coin, a relic from the past, has been given here a second lease of life: "Instead of sitting around in drawers, we have made it into something alive," said Nicola Bulgari (*Playbill*, June 1982).

THE EVOLUTION OF THE BVLGARI STYLE

106. *A necklace set with cabochon emeralds, rubies, sapphires and brillant-cut diamonds (1967-68). An impressive creation showing the favourite Bulgari colour combination of the time. The cabochon cut for the coloured stones is another trademark of the firm.*

107. *A superb bib necklace and a pair of matching earclips, 1965. The striking effect is achieved by juxtaposing precious and semiprecious gemstones of contrasting colours: 35.44 carats of turquoises, 63.31 carats of cabochon emeralds, 51 carats of cabochon amethysts and 38.57 carats of brilliant-cut diamonds. The perfection of the reverse is an indication of its fine workmanship. Note how the reverse of the clasp is decorated with a pierced gold panel of flowerhead design, a decorative feature which in the following years was extended to the entire back of most Bulgari jewels.*

The 1970s

During the 1970s Bulgari's style continued its gradual evolution in increasingly recognisable forms. The stylisation of naturalistic motifs contained within geometric forms, which is a theme central to Bulgari's style, began to take shape. A good example is provided by a sautoir of 1971 (ill. 114) where the pendant, decorated with a stylised flowering plant motif, is contained within an angular seven-sided frame. Such angular forms, characteristic of Bulgari's early 1970s design, contrast with the later, softer and more rounded shapes. A catalyst for this tendency towards stylisation of floral forms was undoubtedly the influence of Egyptian art. This came once again to the forefront of design following the sensational first exhibition of Tutankhamun's treasures in the West in 1972. Stylised lotus motifs in the Egyptian manner are central to two Bulgari necklaces of this period (ill. 111, 112). It is not surprising that Egyptian art provided a

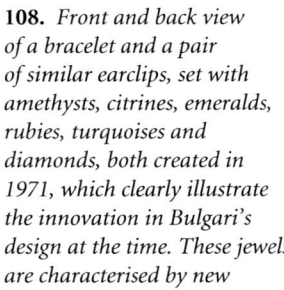

108. Front and back view of a bracelet and a pair of similar earclips, set with amethysts, citrines, emeralds, rubies, turquoises and diamonds, both created in 1971, which clearly illustrate the innovation in Bulgari's design at the time. These jewels are characterised by new features such as volume, contrasting coloured gemstones chosen regardless of their value and stylised floral patterns enclosed in smooth contours. Volume, colour and stylisation, which began to feature in Bulgari jewels from the 1960s, were and continue to be at the heart of the firm's design.

THE EVOLUTION OF THE BVLGARI STYLE

source of inspiration, as its stylisation combined with its strong chromatism matched Bulgari's design philosophy at the time.

It was at this time that Bulgari developed and began exploring two devices which later became trademarks. One consisted of an oval element set with a cabochon gem in a concentric surround of gold, diamonds and, in some cases, enamel. This design was used in numerous variations and adapted to all forms of jewels, but in particular it suited the decoration of longchains which were fashionable at the time (ill. 110). The second device was the thick gold chain of filed curb linking known as *gourmette*. This was used to form bracelets and necklaces of various lengths, at times decorated with the recurring oval element, at times with simpler elements formed by cabochon gems in plain collets. Characteristically, the most frequent palette is of vivid colours: green emeralds, red rubies and blue sapphires (ill. 113).

Besides these innovations, Bulgari also responded to current fashion in their production of jewels of Indian inspiration. Especially during these years numerous French and American jewellers began exploiting motifs of Indian derivation such as the "*boteh*" – Indian leaf motif – or features typical of Indian jewellery such as combination of white, green and red and the use of beads rather than faceted stones. However, when this Indian trend was adopted by Bulgari it always offered an unmistakable Bulgari flavour. For example, the long sautoir set with cabochon rubies and emeralds beads supporting a large emerald fruit carving is clearly of Indian inspiration, but at the same time the *gourmette* chain makes it unmistakably Bulgari (ill. 113). Another fine example is the gem-set sautoir supporting a boteh pendant set with a large carved emerald. In this case Bulgari characteristically stylises the Indian motif by enclosing it in a compact outline and suspends it from a chain of rectangular gem-set links (ill. 115). At times, the firm successfully remounted gemstones which had been part of Indian treasures, such as in the impressive sautoir illustrated at no. 116.

American designer Donald Claflin (1933-1979) joined the firm in 1976. A former designer at Tiffany & Co., Claflin created jewels for

109. *A brooch set with cabochon sapphires and rubies embellished with brilliant-cut diamonds, circa 1970. This colour combination was favoured by Bulgari in particular from 1965 to the early 1970s.*

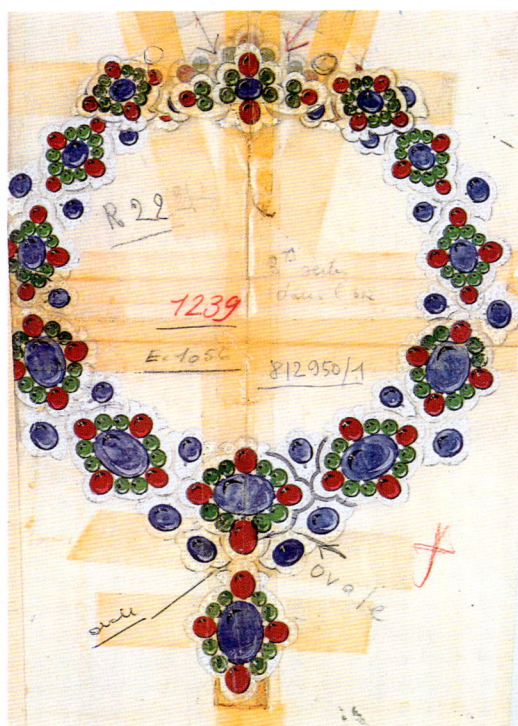

110. Designs for two necklaces, 1963 and 1970 respectively, which illustrate the characteristic use of cabochon gemstones and the emphasis on combination of contrasting colours – red, green and blue.

Bulgari that were formed by clean shapes and smooth contours which embodied the firm's criteria of design. He is best remembered for his successful loop earrings, formed by a continuous line of baguette diamonds, and for his crossover rings.

During these years Bulgari began to use yellow gold more and more. Traditionally silver, platinum and white gold had been the metals associated with formal evening wear, while yellow gold had mainly been confined to informal day-time jewellery. But from now on yellow gold became the favourite metal for setting all jewels, even

111. A bib necklace of 1971 set with turquoises, cabochon amethysts, cabochon emeralds and brilliant-cut diamonds.

THE EVOLUTION OF THE BVLGARI STYLE

112. *A spectacular necklace of 1972, decorated with stylised lotus motifs set with cabochon sapphires, black onyx and salmon pink coral highlighted with diamonds. The stylised floral pattern is of clear Egyptian derivation and illustrates how Bulgari readily responded to cultural phenomena of the time. Egyptian art, design and jewels came to the forefront in the western world in the early 1970s following the sensational first ever exhibition of the treasures of Tutankhamun.*

BVLGARI

those mounted with important gemstones. By doing so Bulgari enabled even extremely important jewels to be worn in a more casual and informal fashion, responding to the climate of the time. Women were now looking for wearable yet sophisticated jewels, which could be worn from morning until night. This development in Bulgari design had been anticipated by Gianni Bulgari who, in an interview in *The New York Post*, 1 September 1970 – on the eve of the opening of a branch in New York – stated: "They [women] no longer want something they put on or carry for great occasions, but jewelry they wear often with many things." The wearable aspect of jewellery was then and continues to be one of the firm's main concerns. As Paolo Bulgari said in 1991, when writing about the *Naturalia* collection: "For a long time I have been trying to create a new line of jewellery, pieces which any woman would desire to wear all day long."

113. *A diamond-set longchain of filed curb linking (gourmette) set with cabochon rubies and emerald beads, supporting a large carved emerald drop. Early 1970s.*

114. *A gold and gem-set sautoir of 1971 decorated with chrysoprase, calibré-cut citrines and amethysts set against a pavé-set diamond ground. It is a good example of how, by this time, naturalistic motifs such as flowers begin to be stylised and contained within characteristically angular contours.*

THE EVOLUTION OF THE BVLGARI STYLE

115. *A striking gem-set sautoir, 1969-70 (and its design), formed by a chain set with cabochon amethysts, citrines, turquoises, emeralds and rubies, with a large carved emerald of 127.40 carats at the front.*

116. *Another impressive sautoir of the 1970s strung with ruby beads and natural pearls supporting an ancient Indian carved emerald drop of 36.97 carats. This jewel was assembled from gems that came to the firm as part of the jewellery collection of the Nizams of Hyderabad, Muslim rulers of fabled wealth, whose authority once extended across much of southern India.*

117. *A gem-set sautoir and its design, 1970. Its vibrant colours combined with the cabochon cut of the stones are typical features of Bulgari creations of this time. Note the pendant reminiscent of Indian motifs.*

95

From 1980s to the 21st Century

"Well, I think your jewellery is the 1980s. Everybody's trying to copy this look," stated Andy Warhol while interviewing Nicola Bulgari. It was, indeed, around 1980 that all those features of design which had been taking shape over the years came together and crystallised into a recognisable form: volume, striking colours, clean shapes, stylised decorative motifs and awareness of antiquity came to form the unmistakable Bulgari style.

That all designs should conform to such canons was not a haphazard event but a conscious decision of centralisation, which enabled Bulgari to spread throughout the world a universal and coherent product. In 1980 Bulgari set up "Bulgari Distribuzione", a company whose sole purpose was to conceive, design, manufacture and distribute jewels and objects to Bulgari outlets world-wide.

This was a turning point both for the creative aspect and for the structural organisation of the company. At the structural level, the innovation insured that all Bulgari creations were not only designed and produced in a uniform manner but also distributed through a network of shops characterised by a consistent image and decor. The creative expansion involved skilled designers from areas far beyond jewellery, such as the car industry, sculpture and architecture. Bulgari realised that this input would be stimulating and beneficial. The methods and techniques used by an industrial designer or an architect when designing or modelling are much more advanced and sophisticated than those used traditionally in jewellery, and are therefore extremely beneficial for the firm. This novel input resulted in one of the company's most fertile periods, which saw the conception and realisation of a number of extremely successful creations. Among these are modular jewels or jewels formed by a repetition of elements devoid of superfluous ornamentation, which interlock in an infinity of combinations and form a recognisable "family" or line of jewellery.

The first modular line of jewels was launched in 1982; it was named *Parentesi,* for the design is reminiscent of stylized brackets (ill. 163-166). At the beginning nobody could have imagined the extraordinary

118. *In 1980 Bulgari introduced a new way of mounting the finest gemstones: not on gold and gem encrusted collars, but on coloured silk cords. These could be supplied in a wide range of colours and changed to complement different coloured outfits. In so doing, Bulgari managed to transform important and expensive ornaments into versatile jewels.* *These designs of 1983 for three cabochon sapphire and diamond necklaces illustrate the ubiquitous transgressive streak of Bulgari creations.*

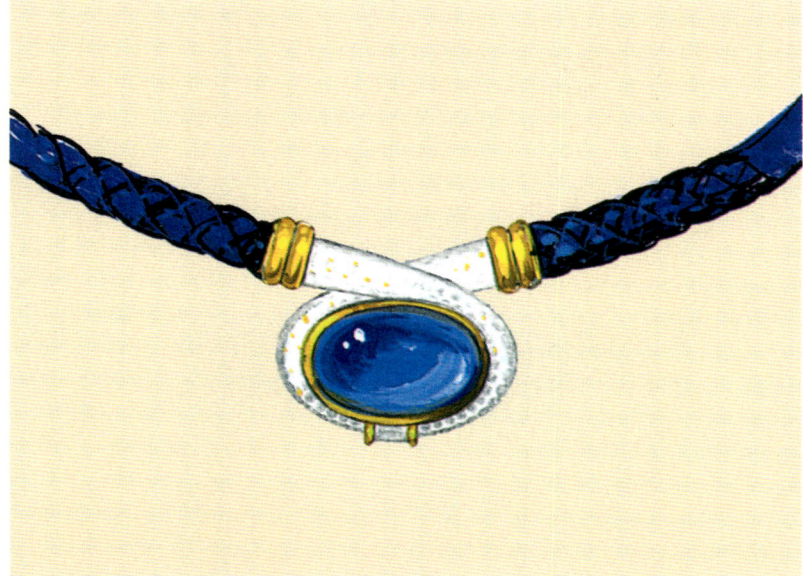

impact of this line, which soon became one of the icons of high jewellery of the decade. To this day, in fact, it remains one of the most copied jewellery designs of all times. From 1982 on Bulgari has continued to capitalise on modular jewels, creating eight additional lines: *Doppio Cuore, Boules, Gancio, Alveare, Saetta, Spiga, Celtica* and *Trika* (ill. 167-173). The common denominator of modular jewels is that they are characterised by bold and recognisable designs consisting of rounded contours and clean shapes, available in a wide price range. All these features contribute to make them highly desirable and wearable. "Wearability" and strong, recognisable shapes are corner-stones of Bulgari's design.

Modular jewels came as a consequence of Bulgari's awareness that the jewellery market had changed drastically. "There is an enormous market for not-too-expensive but well-designed jewellery, but the market is more limited for quality pieces at very high prices," noted Gianni Bulgari in 1981. "We are trying to change our image from one of a business only for the very rich to one designed for those of discerning tastes. You don't have to be rich to like quality" (*International Daily News*, 20-21 September 1981). Bulgari realised that if the intrinsic value of a piece had to be reduced to address a wider audience, design had to be stronger, more inventive and sophisticated to compensate the jewel's relative low value. "*Venendo a mancare, per questioni di costi, la materia prima, cioè pietre preziose e oro, dobbiamo dare almeno un disegno che sia di alta classe e grande raffinatezza*" (Gianni Bulgari in *Gioia*, Milan, 5 April 1982).

In the 1980s came the extraordinary crescendo in popularity of the BVLGARI-BVLGARI wristwatch (ill. 253). Created in 1977, it was conceived as a plain black circular dial encircled by a polished metal frame engraved with the firm's logo. Like all Bulgari creations, this timepiece relies on a plain yet bold shape. Furthermore, it is clearly recognisable as a Bulgari creation due to its inscription which is also used here as a decorative device. As mentioned before, Bulgari's policy from the late 1970s was one of consolidating the idea of recognisable designs, so it is not surprising that its logo too became a key element of the firm's decorative repertoire. This quest for recognisability is

THE EVOLUTION OF THE BVLGARI STYLE

reflected also in the firm's contemporary advertising campaigns which exploited the repetition of the "BVLGARI-BVLGARI" logo as a backdrop for jewels, watches and objects (ill. 279, 280).

The 1980s also saw a further development in the concept of transgression and demystification of jewellery, a concern close to Bulgari's heart and linked to the firm's belief that jewels should not be relegated to the darkness of a vault but rather be worn at all times. As a direct consequence of this quest to create wearable jewels to suit the active and dynamic lifestyle of modern women, Bulgari in 1980 introduced a new way of mounting the finest gems: not on gold and gem encrusted collars but on coloured silk cords (ill. 118-122). These could be supplied in a wide range of colours and changed to complement differently coloured outfits; in this manner Bulgari succeeded in transforming an important and highly expensive gem into a versatile and wearable ornament. This daring combination – priceless gems and worthless cords – had never been employed in high jewellery before, and continued to be used extensively until 1985.

Always motivated by the concept that a jewel is a work of art regardless of the intrinsic value of its gems, Bulgari increased the juxtaposition of extremely precious and costly gems with comparatively worthless stones: emeralds with amethysts and rubies with citrines (ill. 203). The Bulgari are known to have said: "We don't want women to look like traffic lights or Christmas trees. We're understated, blending the formal and the casual."

119. *Designs of 1984 for two necklaces mounted on silk cords and set with cabochon sapphires, cabochon rubies and diamonds.*

99

THE EVOLUTION OF THE BVLGARI STYLE

120. *The combination of silk cord and precious gemstones was amongst the most successful innovations of Bulgari in the early 1980s. This is confirmed by the frequent presence of such ornaments in the advertising campaigns between 1983 and 1985.*

This disregard for the intrinsic value of the gems in favour of an appreciation for novel colour combinations is a feature that especially dominates the design of jewels and ornaments of the *Bulgari Collection Internationale – "BCI"*. This consists of a collection of unique pieces of jewellery and objects mounted with exceptionally fine gems, which are displayed in rotation in all Bulgari outlets world-wide.

The necessity of creating such a collection of unique jewels conceived as show pieces of Bulgari's creativity arose in 1980 in response to the growing expansion of the firm. In particular, the designer Omar Torres (b. 1945), who worked with the firm from 1979 until 1994, was instrumental in the success of the bold, colourful and striking *Bulgari*

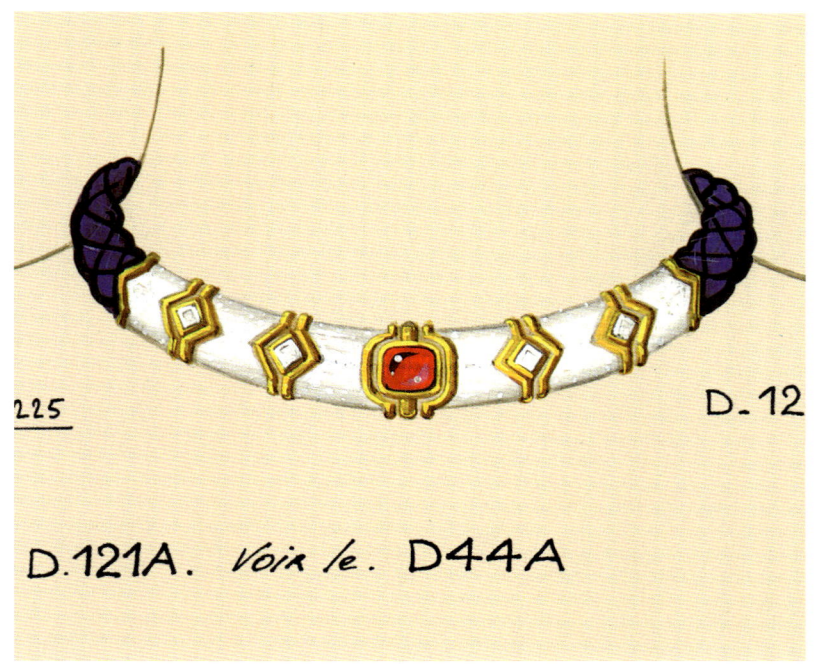 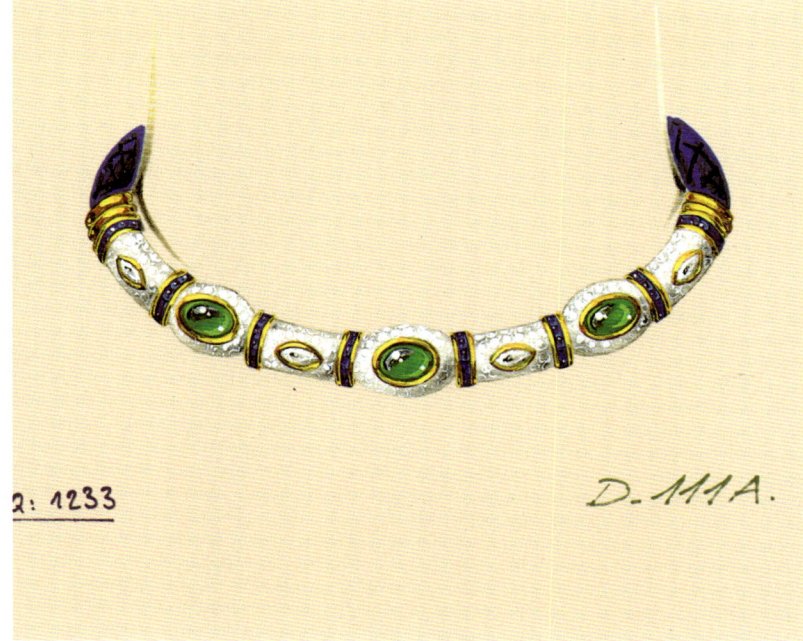

Collection Internationale jewels of this period, which are characterised by soft and rounded shapes. Torres softened in fact the hard-edged Bulgari jewels of the 1970s: "I have a greater use of curved lines," he said, "I can't picture jewels without seeing the curves of the ears and the cheekbones" (*Palm Beach Daily News*, 20 May 1981).

The consistent high quality of these pieces is a combination of fine craftsmanship and a painstaking search for the ultimate stones. The exceptional quality of the workmanship is guaranteed by the enduring co-operation of workshops such as the one of Crescenzi, which continues to be managed by Ubaldo's daughters, Nunzi and Marina. The perfect combination of fine gemstones is the result of a laborious

121. *Two designs of 1983 and 1984 for necklaces mounted on silk ropes and set respectively with a cabochon ruby and three cabochon emeralds.*

122. *Necklaces mounted on silk cords were at the zenith of popularity between 1983 and 1985. These two examples from 1983 and 1984 are respectively set with a cabochon sapphire and a heart-shaped yellow sapphire, both within diamond surrounds.*

and lengthy search throughout international gem markets. This involves a ruthless process of elimination of stones that do not conform to the high standards of the *Bulgari Collection Internationale*. As Bulgari approaches the 21st century it continues to be faithful to its principles of quality of design and workmanship. At the same time the firm renews itself by responding to current concerns such as attention to the environment.

In this respect Paolo Bulgari said: "Finally, I have found the inspiration in Nature. The result is a line of jewellery called *Naturalia*, which seeks to represent a tribute to Nature's beauty and richness with a metaphorical representation of natural objects."

Naturalia, a collection of jewellery based on stylised naturalistic motifs ranging from flowers and plants to birds and fish, a collection conceived as a celebration of nature, was launched in 1991 (ill. 123,

206). This environmental concern was not purely theoretical but was proved by Bulgari's association with the World Wide Fund for Nature in support of the Biological Diversity Campaign. Paolo Bulgari said in 1991: "We have chosen to support WWF because we feel that the inspiration behind the *Naturalia* jewels and the themes of the Campaign have an important common point: they are both invitations to a rediscovery of nature in its purest sense and celebration of its forms, colours and richness." Bulgari's support for the WWF included the creation of the film *Anima Mundi*, which was used as the campaign's visual manifesto, and culminated in a charity auction of fourteen *Naturalia* jewels at Sotheby's Geneva.

The idea of transgression and novelty continues to thrive at Bulgari. In 1994 the *Chandra* collection was first presented (ill. 125, 126). This innovative and provocative line of jewels is rendered in white, smooth porcelain moulded into variously shaped beads and curved elements decorated in relief. These are combined with gold, and precious and colourful gems to create a variety of pieces ranging from necklaces to earrings, bracelets and rings. The collection was launched with a sensational party held at Bulgari in Paris, immortalised in the film *Prêt-à-Porter* (directed by Robert Altman) where movie stars mingled with socialites and celebrities of the fashion world. The name *Chandra* – Sanskrit for Moon – was chosen for the association between the whiteness of porcelain and that of the Moon. The qualities of this material, unusual in jewellery, inspired Paolo Bulgari: "I wanted to create jewels that were different, fun and transgressive," he said. "Porcelain, which is luminous and smooth, fascinated me: it carries with it an ancient and elegant history but it is modern and wearable at all times" (*Allure*, Italy, June 1994).

On the eve of 21st century Bulgari shows no sign of faltering but, on the contrary, continues to thrive and expand as never before: a firm that has been flourishing for four generations is as alive, as creative and as unpredictable as ever. As Nicola Bulgari says, "You cannot simply live on past glories; that's foolish. To be a success, you have to combine the worlds of the past, present and the future. That is the challenge, and there are many horizons" (*Palm Beach Daily News*, January 1995).

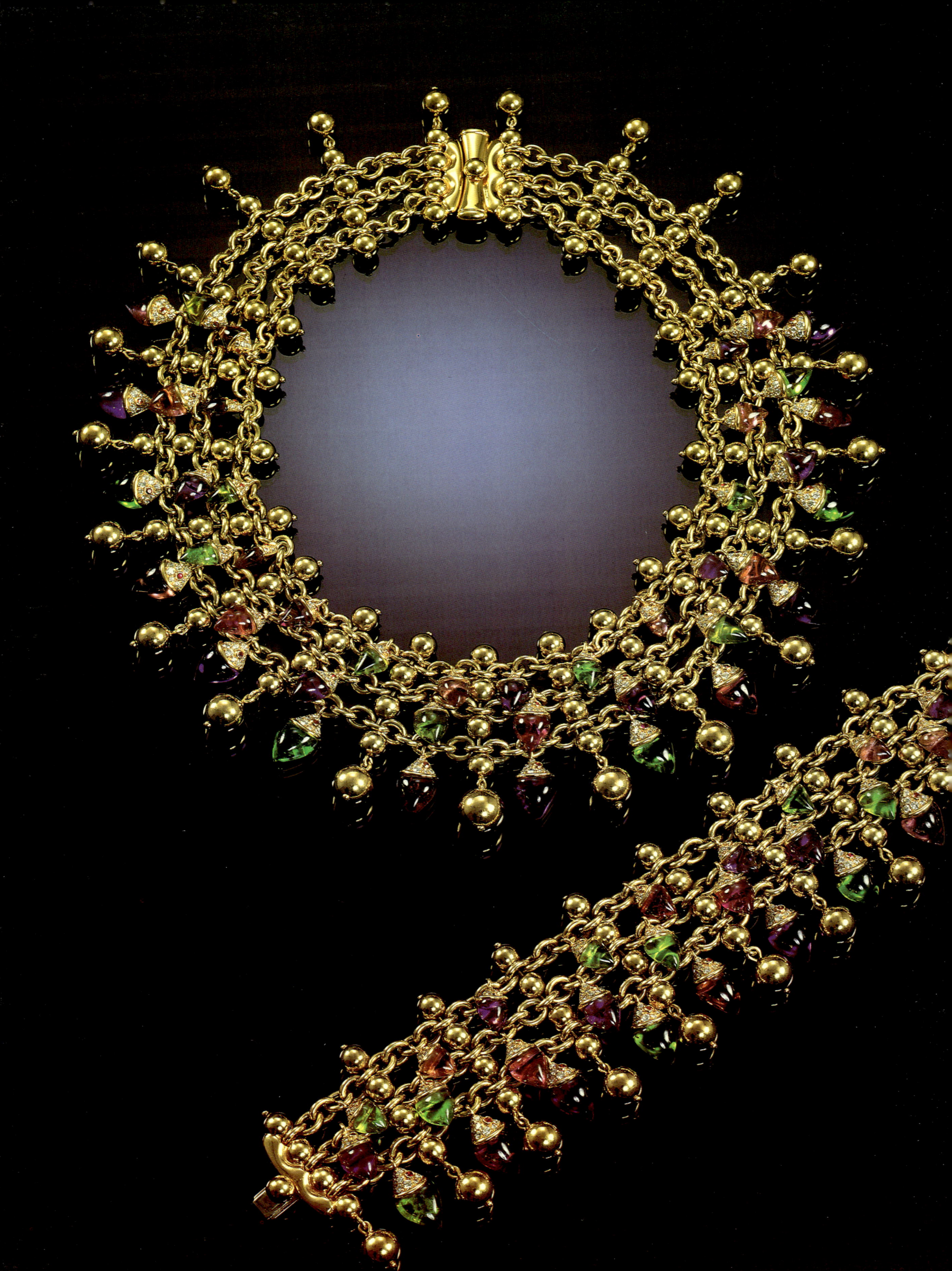

THE EVOLUTION OF THE BVLGARI STYLE

123. *A gold and gem-set necklace and matching bracelet from the* Naturalia *collection of 1991. The tiny fish suspended from gold chains are carved in pink tourmalines, peridots and amethysts and have diamond heads set with ruby eyes.*

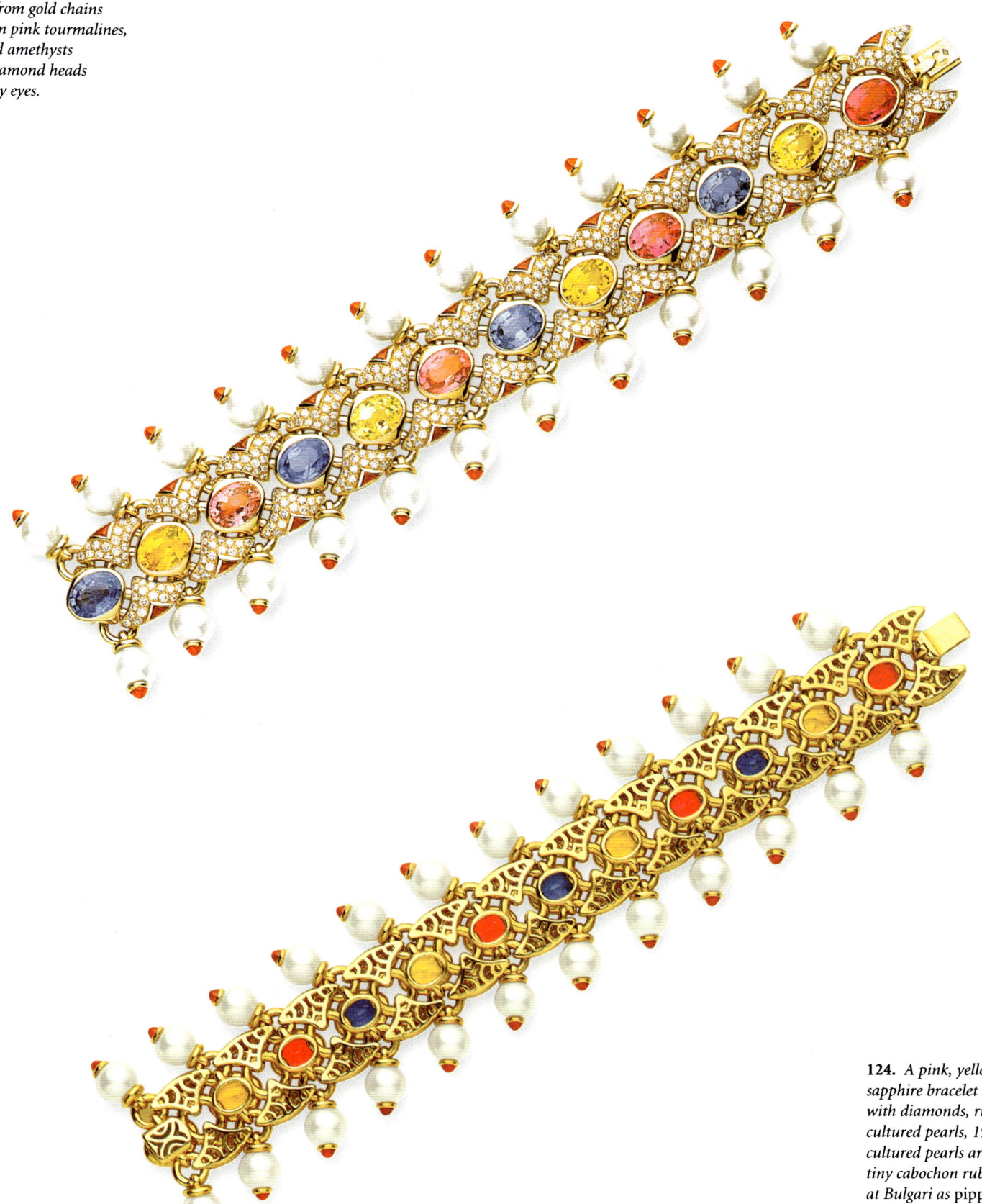

124. *A pink, yellow and blue sapphire bracelet decorated with diamonds, rubies and cultured pearls, 1994. The cultured pearls are tipped with tiny cabochon rubies, known at Bulgari as* pippoli. *This term refers to small cabochon coloured stones which Bulgari used, from the early 1980s, to edge, punctuate and trim its jewels. The reverse illustrates the use of the* griglia, *a pierced metal backing to the jewel, which echoes the decorative motif of the front.*

125. *A necklace from the* Chandra *collection of 1994. The white porcelain beads are suspended from a gold chain decorated with pink tourmalines and peridots. The luminous smoothness of white porcelain inspired Paolo Bulgari to combine this material with gemstones. Interviewed on this subject he said: "I wanted to create jewels that were different, fun and transgressive."*

126. *The model Brandi wearing* Chandra *necklaces and earrings, 1994.*

BVLGARI

127. Celtica *jewels of 1993 were inspired by Celtic bronze bracelets or anklets dating to the 3rd century BC. This selection includes a gold necklace, set with semiprecious stones (citrines, amethysts, tourmalines, topazes and garnets) and two similarly decorated rings embellished with brilliant-cut diamonds.*

The Use of Coins

Coins in Ancient Times

In the Western world, official state coinage dates back to the second half of the 7th century BC. By the beginning of that century, the most common means of exchange for important transactions consisted of silver or gold ingots. These were gradually replaced by lenticular beads of electrum (a natural alloy of gold and silver) of standard weight. In order to guarantee the metal and its weight, individual merchants and religious sanctuaries started to stamp these lenticular beads with their own marks. Around the middle of the 7th century, States intervened and started to apply their official stamps to these lenticular beads, providing a more universal guarantee. This gave birth to coinage in much the same form as is used today. Its success was such that it spread rapidly from Ionian Greece (modern Turkey) throughout the Mediterranean world.

By the 6th century BC, Greek coins were mainly made of silver and bore on one side the emblem of the city where they had been coined. The decorations could be the effigy of the local deity or its attributes, or any symbol connected to a local cult, agricultural produce, or toponymy. In early Greek coinage the legend was always very short, often an abbreviation of the name of the city-state where the coin had been struck.

From the reign of Alexander the Great (336-323 BC), Hellenistic coinage came to be decorated with the portrait of the ruler and a more extensive legend including the ruler's name, his title, and the location of coinage. The beauty and excellence achieved in ancient Greek coinage is outstanding and has never been surpassed. Indeed, the design and execution is so fine that these ancient coins can be regarded as works of art in their own right; this artistic value was

128. *Advertising, 1975-80.*

129. *Silver stater of Metapontum, depicting an ear of barley, circa 500 BC.*

130. *Electrum hekte of Lesbos, 4th century BC.*

131. *Gold aureus of Augustus (27 BC-AD 14).*

132. *Silver Siculo-Punic tetradrachm depicting the profile of Kore-Persephone, 4th century BC.*

133. *Silver tetradrachm of Alexander the Great (336-323 BC).*

134. *Roman Republican silver didrachm, 225-212 BC.*

135. *Silver stater, Corinth, circa 350 BC.*

137. *Syracusan bronze of the 3rd century BC.*

138. *Bronze coin, Carthage, 3rd century BC.*

136. *Bronze Domitian as (AD 81-96).*

also appreciated in antiquity. So much so that in Sicily individual artists such as Euainetos, Phrygillos, Eukleidas and Kimon, who designed the famous coins from Syracuse with Arethusa, were allowed to sign them.

It is matter of debate when the first true Roman silver coin, the *denarius*, with its bronze sub-multiples (*quinarius*, *sestertius*), was struck. According to Livy and Pliny the Elder, this occurred in 268 BC. Roman coins are characterised by a greater variety of decorative motifs compared to the earlier Greek examples, but are lower in artistic quality. In the 1st century BC, the depiction of Julius Caesar's head prompted the subsequent production of an endless series of coins bearing the image of living rulers, which were also used at the time as political propaganda. It is around this time that a gold coin, the *aureus*, extremely rare in the Republican period, began to be

139. *Electrum hektes, Phokaia, 5th-4th century BC.*

circulated extensively. Continuing the imagery of silver coinage, *aurei* became a gallery of gold Imperial portraiture. It is interesting that the custom of depicting the image of a ruler on coinage has never subsided and continues today.

Ever since antiquity, coins have been collected for their rarity and for their artistic value. They have also been mounted in jewellery at intervals throughout history. In Ancient Rome, from the end of the 1st century AD, Imperial gold coins were frequently mounted in jewels (ill. 144). They formed the centrepiece of rings, brooches and necklaces, where they assumed a prominent position often framed by intricate gold fretwork. This characteristic fretwork is illustrated by a brooch (ill. 144) dating from the 3rd century AD, which is mounted with an *aureus* of Philip I (AD 244-249). Clearly, when these coins went out of circulation, their being selected was

141. *Didrachm, Naples, 4th century BC.*

142. *Electrum stater, Carthage, circa 280 BC.*

140. *Bronze coin, Syracuse, Agathocles (317-289 BC).*

THE USE OF COINS

143. *Three Anglo-Saxon pendants mounted with gold coins within garnet cloisonné frames dating from the 7th century AD. These examples demonstrate how the taste of the time favoured elaborate frames for coins, respectively a solidus of Valentinian II (AD 375-392), a solidus of Heraclius I and Constantine – the latter mounted upside down with the reverse showing on the front of the jewel – and a solidus of Valens (AD 364-378).*

144. *Two Roman gold rings, 3rd century AD, respectively set with an aureus of Caracalla (AD 211 or 198?-217) and with an aureus of Emperor Elagabalus (AD 218-222). Often such rings mounted with coins portraying an emperor were given as gifts with the purpose of political propaganda. The third jewel, a brooch from the 3rd century AD, is mounted with an aureus of Philip I (AD 244-249) within an elaborate gold fret-work typical of late Roman and Byzantine jewels.*

145. *Part of a gold chain dating to the 6th-7th century AD, each link set with a solidus of Justinian I (AD 527-565).*

It is interesting to observe that jewels mounted with multiple coins were rare in antiquity.

115

146. *Two gold bracelets (Italian, circa 1870) mounted with ancient silver coins. The above example is set with six ancient Greek coins: an Athenian tetradrachm (4th century BC), a tetradrachm of Attalus I of Pergamum (241-197 BC), a tetradrachm of Alexander the Great (336-323 BC), a Syracusan 16 litrae of Queen Philistis, wife of Hieron II (274-215 BC), and a Syracusan tetradrachm of Agathocles (317-289 BC), a Syracusan tetradrachm (circa 480 BC). The smaller bracelet is set with eight denarii of the Roman Republic, 2nd-1st century BC, including one of Julius Caesar, all in simple gold corded wire mounts.*

solely based on their decorative potential. When they were still in current usage, they were imbued with a political message, either of propaganda or allegiance. For example, it is possible that rings with imperial coins were awarded as military distinctions. This fashion continued to flourish in Europe until the late 7th century AD and was particularly popular in the Byzantine and Anglo-Saxon worlds. Fine examples are exhibited in the British Museum collection (ill. 143, 145).

Coins in 19th-Century Jewellery

In the second half of the 19th century ancient coins again played a prominent role in jewellery. This coincided with a general interest in reviving ancient designs and techniques prompted by the numerous archaeological discoveries of the time. In particular, the Roman jeweller Castellani and his circle very successfully exploited the decorative value of ancient coins, incorporating them in jewels in the "archaeological revival" style (ill. 146-148). When mounting ancient Greek and Roman coins, Castellani treated them as true gems. He appreciated their decorative value and above all he aimed to establish a continuity with the past by bringing antiquity to life again. This was the ultimate manifestation of historicism; not only looking to the past

THE USE OF COINS

for inspiration but incorporating a genuine fragment of antiquity in a modern context. Thus Castellani and his contemporaries gave coins, used in ancient times mainly for commercial transactions, a further lease on life as jewels.

In general, 19th-century archaeological revivalist jewellers used silver specimens such as Hellenistic *tetradrachm* and Roman *denarii*, which were abundant in archaeological finds in Italy at the time. These were clearly chosen for their appealing design; particularly beautiful coins show the head of Alexander the Great, the goddess Roma, and the nymph Arethusa. In addition, the contrast between the ancient silver patina and the modern matt gold mount was always employed to great effect. The 19th-century mounts, however, were fairly plain, decorated if at all with beaded work which offset the beauty of the coin. This rendering differed from that of late Roman, Byzantine and Anglo-Saxon jewels, where the elaborate pierced work or garnet inlay used to frame the coin tended to overshadow its inherent beauty. Furthermore, when coins were mounted as jewels in antiquity they were always made of gold, which suggests that the preciousness of the metal was more important than the decoration of the coin.

In general, 19th-century interest in coins as archaeological heritage is further highlighted by the fact that even irregularly shaped or

147. A gold demi parure by Roccheggiani (Rome, circa 1880). The brooch is mounted with Macedonian tetradrachms including one of Philip II (359-336 BC) and one of Alexander the Great (336-323 BC). The earrings are set with Roman Republican denarii of the 1st century BC.

148. A gold brooch by Castellani (circa 1865), mounted with a denarius of L. Plautius Plancus (circa 47 BC). It is interesting to note how the 19th-century jeweller respected the ancient coin by not concealing its imperfections. Castellani also played on the contrast between the different colours of the metals – a feature central to Bulgari coin jewels a century later.

149. *A necklace of the 1970s formed by alternate clusters of cabochon emeralds and rubies within diamond borders. This illustrates a typical form of Bulgari setting adopted both for precious gems and ancient coins.*

THE USE OF COINS

damaged examples were chosen and that the mounts did not conceal these imperfections. An example of this is the gold mounted *denarius* (L. Plautius Plancus, circa 47 BC) brooch by Castellani where the uneven outline of the corroded coin is not concealed by its delicate circular frame (ill. 148).

With the decline of the fashion for archaeological revival jewellery at the end of the century, coins mounted as gems disappeared from the fashionable lady's casket for over half a century.

Bulgari's "Gemme Nummarie"

In the mid 1960s it was Bulgari who resumed the long-standing tradition of setting ancient coins in jewellery. The beginning of this trend, which is one of the most recognisable trademarks of the firm, was initially almost accidental. Nicola Bulgari began by setting coins in small brooches. He had always been a keen coin collector – his interest had been aroused by his godfather, Ubaldo Crescenzi, who gave him ancient Roman coins to mark his wedding anniversaries. Perhaps the silver jewels set by Sotirio in the late 19th century with *faux* coins also served as inspiration (ill. 57).

After some initial attempts, Bulgari began mounting long chains of filed curb linking with various coins, which were received with great

150. *A gold and diamond chain necklace of the late 1960s, set at the front with an* orichalcum *semis, an* aureus *and a* denarius *of Nero (AD 54-68). By framing the coins with diamonds Bulgari is treating them just like precious gems. This setting is almost identical to that of the cabochon gemstones in the necklace illustrated opposite. Furthermore, this necklace relies on a successful play of colour of the three different metals the coins are made of: brass, gold and silver.*

THE USE OF COINS

151. A gold and diamond necklace of the early 1980s. By mounting fragments of antiquity Bulgari is continuing a well-established tradition, with a completely modern and original result. This aspect highlights Bulgari's great talent: whilst working with the same ingredients as ancient Romans and their 19th-century predecessors, Bulgari does not imitate them. On the contrary, it adds novel and inspiring input to a well-established tradition. Observe how the classical profile portrayed on the coin contrasts with the sleek, modern design and setting of the necklace. The gold chain is set with a South-Italian stater of the 3rd century BC within a surround of diamonds.

enthusiasm by the firm's clientele. From then on Bulgari has not stopped mounting ancient coins in its jewels. These fragments of antiquity are treated with the same reverence as gems of great value, to the extent that coins are referred to by Bulgari as *Gemme Nummarie* (Coin Gems) (ill. 150-160).

The reason these apparently insignificant gifts have had such enormous consequences for the development of Bulgari style is that the use of coins in the context of jewellery in many ways reflects the firm's aspirations. Bulgari has always been proud of its origins, rooted in the classical Greek tradition and enhanced by Roman culture. By using ancient Greek and Roman coins in modern pieces of jewellery Bulgari is making overt reference to its Hellenic origins grafted in Rome. This confirms the attention to its cultural heritage and the necessity of continuity with the past – an idea which is very dear to the heart of Bulgari.

By mounting ancient coins as gems Bulgari is continuing a well-established tradition; the result, however, is completely modern and original. Even when working with the same ingredients as the ancient Romans and 19th-century jewellers, Bulgari's great talent is to never plagiarise. On the contrary, Bulgari adds a novel and inspiring input to this long tradition of jewellery.

152. *A gold and diamond chain necklace of 1966, mounted with three solidi respectively of Justinian I (AD 527-565), Justinian II (AD 565-578), and Leo I (AD 457-473). Another example of how Bulgari, by framing ancient coins with diamonds, elevates these relics of antiquity to the status of precious gems.*

THE USE OF COINS

The range of coins used by Bulgari is much more varied than that used in the 19th century. It includes bronze, silver, gold and electrum examples from the ancient Mediterranean world as well as European and American coins spanning from the 5th century BC to the 20th century. The reason for this variety can be explained in terms of greater availability of coins on the market, and by the development of numismatics as a science in its own right. Numismatics developed at the beginning of the 20th century when coinage began to be studied and classified in a systematic manner and appreciated as an invaluable historical source. Naturally selection of gem-coins by Bulgari is based on their inherent beauty. Favoured images include those with heads – mainly in profile – of the goddess Roma in armour, Alexander the Great, Medusa, Athena, Arethusa and the Caesars; less frequent are those with other forms of decoration such as the owl attribute of Athena or the ears of wheat of Metapontum.

The coins are mainly set in frames designed as either a single or a double border of gold (ill. 154, 155). The circular structure remains unaltered and is incorporated in a multiplicity of jewels ranging from rings to necklaces, from earrings to bracelets, and also in decorative objects such as boxes, paperknives, ashtrays, bowls and cups (ill. 158, 160). This standard formula of coin and circular setting is then successfully inserted into a wide range of typical Bulgari elements and motifs. Coins are mounted on chains of filed curb linking (ill. 153), applied to flattened or tubular sections of *Tubogas* (ill. 154, 176), suspended from silk cords, and inserted in typical Bulgari modules such as the *Parentesi*. The circular form of coins blends very successfully with the rounded shapes favoured by Bulgari for both outlines and details of their jewels. This emphasis on rounded shapes

THE USE OF COINS

153. *A gold necklace of curb linking set at the front with a silver crown of Queen Elizabeth I (1558-1603). From the mid-1960s on, Bulgari decorated its jewels with coins of different dates ranging from antiquity to the 18th century. The combination of antique and modern, the play of metals' contrasting colours has become one of the firm's trademarks.*

has been a feature of Bulgari jewellery since the late 1970s in particular. Prior to this time, the circular coin-setting structure tended to be associated with much more angular shapes (ill. 156).

The common denominator among Bulgari jewels mounted with coins is their constant and successful play of contrasts: the contrast in texture between the worn, matt finish of the ancient coin and the sleek, polished, highly reflective surface of the modern surround; the contrast in colour between the metal of the coin and the metal of the mount – silver, bronze, gold, electrum and steel; and, of course, the contrast between the antique object and the modern framework.

Bulgari always respects the ancient coin. Like its 19th-century

154. *A Roman denarius depicting Augustus (27 BC - AD 14) inset on a three coloured gold* Tubogas *bracelet of the 1980s. Note the successful contrast between the polished gold and the patina of the ancient coin.*

predecessors, Bulgari does not conceal a coin's irregularities or signs of wear. The sleek modern mounts frequently follow the irregular contours of a worn or poorly struck coin (ill. 176). Furthermore, the Bulgari setting for coins is constructed in such a way that it never damages the ancient specimen and does not debase its inherent numismatic value. This aspect demonstrates once again Bulgari's reverence for antiquity.

This extreme appreciation for the antique and scholarly approach to numismatics leads Bulgari to research each individual coin and inscribe the reverse of its mount with relevant name, nominal value and year of issue (ill. 153). As always at Bulgari, the characters used for

THE USE OF COINS

155. *A variety of jewels dating from the late 1970s to 1995 including rings, earclips and cufflinks all mounted with ancient silver coins and engraved semiprecious stones from the Mediterranean world. Note how the form of the coins lends itself to decorate the bezel of rings and the centre of earclips.*

156. *Two gold chain and gem-set necklaces (circa 1970). Each is decorated at the front with an angular shield shaped panel respectively inset with a silver tetradrachm of Augustus from Antioch within a baguette and brilliant-cut diamond cruciform motif, and a gold stater of Alexander the Great surrounded by blue enamel and brilliant-cut diamonds. Angular surrounds framing circular coins are a distinctive feature of Bulgari production of the 1970s.*

these inscriptions are copied from Roman epigraphy. In some cases, so that the beauty of the coin can be appreciated in its completeness, the coin is mounted on pivots which allow it to be worn – and therefore viewed – on both sides.

The meticulous selection and purchase of these *Gemme Nummarie* is not underestimated by Bulgari; on the contrary, it is the responsibility of specialists whose sole task is to comb the international coin market in order to find suitable "gems" for these ornaments.

American coins came to the forefront of Bulgari production in particular in 1976. They were chosen by the firm to adorn jewels and objects bearing patriotic imagery designed for the commemoration of the bicentennial of the American Revolution. Early American dollar coins were combined with stars and stripes, rendered in polychrome enamel or rubies, sapphires and diamonds.

THE USE OF COINS

Besides coins, engraved gems such as cameos and intaglios, Roman micromosaics and *commessi* (cameos formed of more than one semiprecious stone), generally of antiquarian subjects, are also mounted by Bulgari (ill. 159). This too is a tradition which began in antiquity, was kept alive in the Renaissance and was revisited in the 19th century. The range of carved stones mounted by Bulgari is quite large, spanning from ancient Greek and Roman specimens to fine 18th-century Neo-classical and 19th-century examples. Their treatment is similar to that of coin-gems, though not as frequent. It is interesting to note that Bulgari has also mounted some of the intaglios that formerly were part of the notorious Poniatowsky Collection. This vast collection, comprising 2601 engraved gems, had been assembled mainly by Prince Stanislaw Poniatowsky (1754-1833) in Italy. After his death, the collection was sold and the antiquity of most of the gems began to be questioned; this gave rise to long and acrimonious controversy. It is now known for certain that Poniatowsky employed famous engravers of his time such as Pichler, Cades, Soletti, Cerbara and possibly Girometti to imitate the ancient Greek masters. These 19th-century artists engraved their cornelian and amethyst gems mainly with classical imagery and signed them in Greek lettering with fictitious names such as ΑΠΟΛΛΩΝΙΔΟΥ, ΓΝΑΙΟΣ, ΠΕΡΓΑΜΟΥ and ΚΡΩΜΟU, with a clear intent to deceive.

157. *A bracelet (1990s) of gold filed curb linking set with two Greek hemidrachms of the 3rd century BC, and a Seleucid drachm.*

Bulgari's most striking creations include an exceptional Julio-Claudian *commesso* in lapis lazuli and marble depicting Tiberius (Roman emperor between AD 14 and 37) formerly in the illustrious Bessborough, Marlborough and Bachstitz collections (ill. 159). Once again the ancient and the modern are combined successfully, with a contrast between the softer lines of the ancient carving and the sharper ones of the modern filed curb linking chain. The whole is offset by the unobtrusive, yet effective, brilliance of diamonds. The result is a truly magnificent 20th-century creation which gives new life to an antique specimen housed for centuries in collectors' cabinets. Undoubtedly among the most striking and recognisable of Bulgari

159. *A Julio-Claudian* commesso *in lapis lazuli and marble depicting the Roman Emperor Tiberius (AD 14-37) mounted by Bulgari in the early 1980s at the centre of a gold chain of filed curb linking. Once again the ancient and the modern are combined successfully, here relying on the contrast between the softer lines of the ancient carving and the sharper ones of the modern chain. The final result is a truly magnificent 20th-century creation which gives new life to an antique specimen, housed for centuries in collectors' cabinets.*

158. *A gold evening bag of 1978, decorated in a honeycomb pattern and set with three tetradrachms of Alexander the Great (336-323 BC). Note the texture contrast between the polished and matt gold and Bulgari's versatile use of coins.*

160. *Coins have been included also in the decoration of objects such as paper-knives, cups, trays and boxes. In this example of 1976, the front of the silver box is inset with Roman Republican and Imperial coins – denarii of Pompeus the Great, Julius Caesar, Cleopatra, Tiberius, Nero and Agrippina, Claudius, with an aureus of Augustus at the centre. Each is mounted in a simple gold frame surmounted by a truncated Doric column. The lid is decorated with four maps of the Mediterranean area depicting the expansion of Rome and its Empire in four stages.*

trademarks is the combination of ancient coins in a modern framework. As Nicola Bulgari stated in the *Palm Beach Daily News* (21 January 1995): "We are very reverent of the past, and inspiration is a magnificent thing, but you must translate these into something that's today and even tomorrow to make a success." Bulgari's prolific production of coin-gem jewels and their extraordinary success can be explained in numerous ways. On one level, the use of ancient Greek and Roman coins matches Bulgari's aspirations in keeping alive their family cultural heritage. On a more universal level, respect for tradition, for the antique and classical past, is one of the main concerns of the Post-modernist movement of the second half of the

20th century. Amongst the aims of Post-modernism is the creation of a modern structure taking into account tradition, cultural context and classical heritage. This aspiration is best exemplified by architecture, where a modern building relies on elements of classical derivation such as pediments, cornices and fluted columns. Such features are clearly reflected in all Bulgari creations which make use of fragments of antiquity in their design, such as the *Gemme Nummarie*. The symbiosis between antique and modern may be taken as the stylistic hallmark of Post-modernism. This confirms that one can never view jewellery in isolation; it is connected to and reflects the much wider cultural, artistic and social trends of its time.

161. *Detail of a Post-modern building (1979-83) in Paris by Ricardo Bofill. The architect has incorporated into this modern structure decorative elements of Classical derivation – columns, metopes and triglyphs – in the same manner that Bulgari incorporates ancient coins in its sleek and modern jewels.*

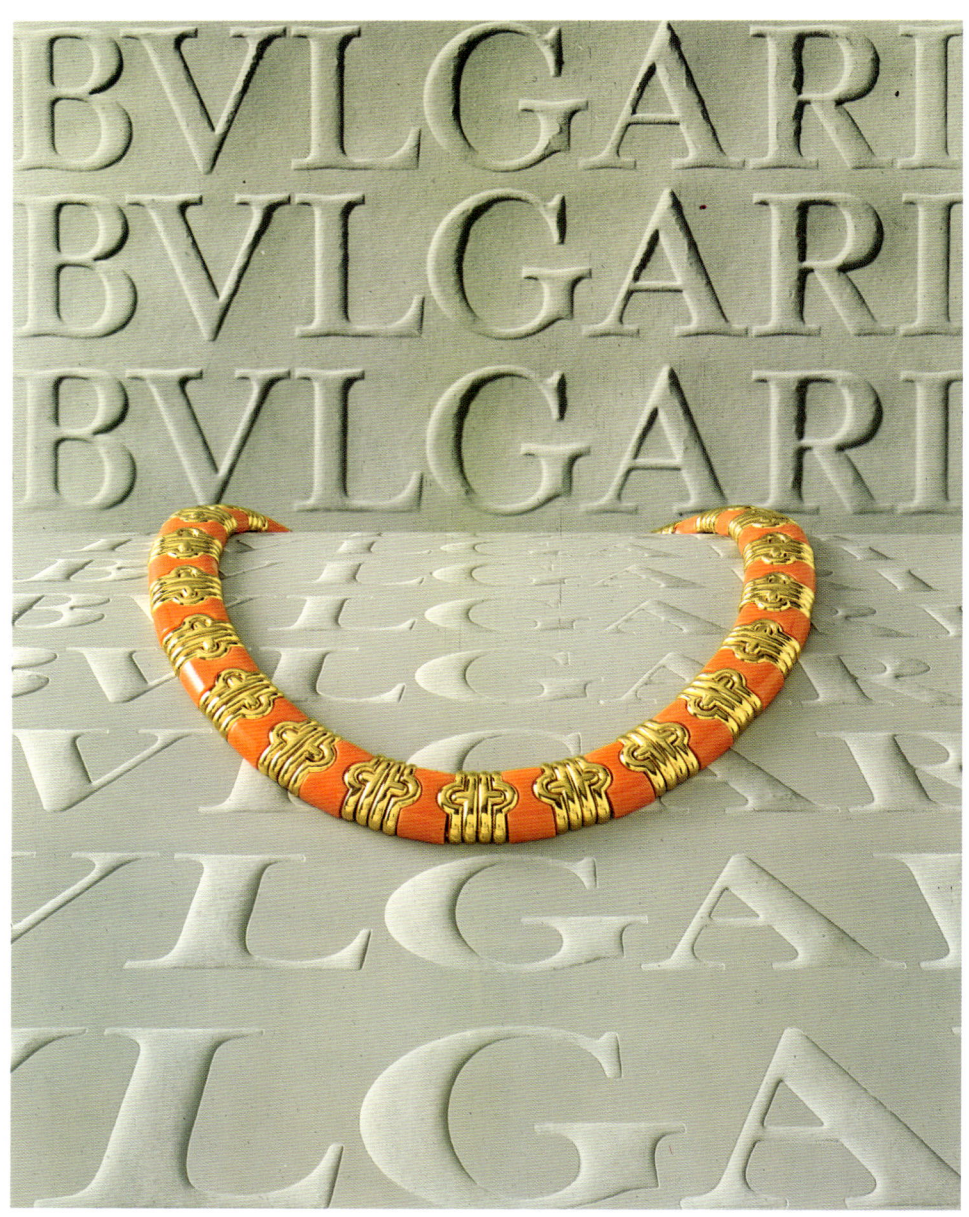

The Power of Bvlgari Design

The "Parentesi"

For Bulgari, the *modulo* (module) is an element of a well-defined shape, free of unnecessary ornamentation, which can be reproduced in series and combined to form a variety of homogeneous designs. The module *Parentesi* (parenthesis) has become the icon of high jewellery in the 1980s (ill. 162). According to statistics, it has been, and still is, one of the most copied designs of all times. To be imitated, however, is a sign of achievement. Nicola Bulgari noted: "If you're copied, it's a good sign. If you're not copied, that's when you should be worried" (*Palm Beach Daily News*, 21 January 1995).

It all began one winter's morning in Rome. The Bulgari team of designers had gathered and were discussing the very nature of inspiration for jewellery design. Some maintained that inspiration must be nurtured and constructed, as it derives mainly from former artistic movements. Others disagreed, arguing that the design of a successful jewel could also be inspired by a graphic sign, chosen at random. Whilst speaking, Gianni Bulgari was doodling and, to demonstrate the latter theory, began drawing a succession of brackets: double, square and round. The potential of this graphic pattern, commonly used in algebra, suddenly became apparent and later its stylised rendering became the core element of a module. After a lengthy process of trial and error, designs and prototypes, this succession of straight and curved interlocking elements took shape in 1982, giving birth to the modular *Parentesi* line of jewels (ill. 163-166). In terms of production, each module is cast in series by a method known as "microfusion." The individual elements are then connected to one another either by means of an interlocking mechanism of hinges or by being strung on a system of chains. The final result is

162. *Advertisement, 1982-85.*

163. *This selection of Parentesi gold, steel and diamond jewels illustrates how the modular element can be adapted to all jewels. It can be used either singularly to form the central element of a ring or repeated many times to form bracelets, earclips and wristwatches.*

similar in either case, the first resulting in jewels that are structurally very secure, the second in more flexible ones.

By far the greatest advantage of the module format is that each single element can be produced in series, at reasonable cost, finished by hand and then assembled in a variety of combinations. It is interesting to note that these modules, though machine-made, are carefully finished by hand involving up to 50% of the total manufacturing process. The quality of the finish, which depends largely on skilled hand labour, is always a prime concern at Bulgari.

Another great asset of the module is that it can be adapted to all jewels. For example, it can be used either singularly to form the central element of a ring, or repeated many times to form a necklace (ill. 163-165). The initial effort made to achieve a successful and satisfactory design is counterbalanced by the possibility for using it repeatedly in other jewels and formats.

Parentesi modules are combined artfully in a gamut of possibilities. The standard format, which consists of gold *Parentesi* motifs alternating with gold connecting elements, can be made more precious by encrusting one of the two parts with diamonds (ill. 163, 166). Similarly the jewel can be made less precious by alternating gold *Parentesi* motifs with connecting elements either of steel, haematite,

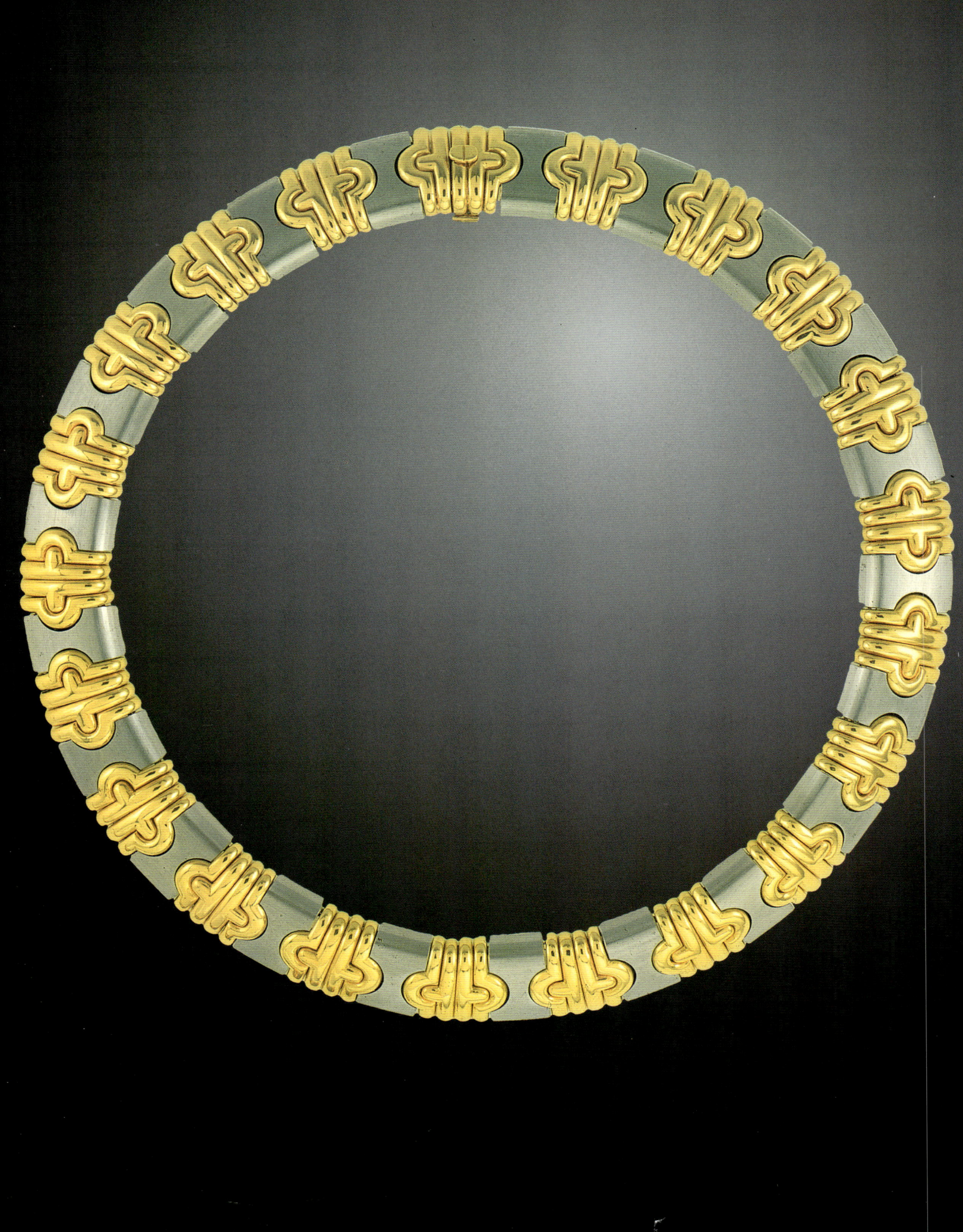

THE POWER OF BVLGARI DESIGN

164. *A gold and steel* Parentesi *necklace.*

165. *A gold and red coral* Parentesi *necklace. Both examples illustrate how the repetition of the modular* Parentesi *motif is successfully employed on large-scale ornaments rendered in diverse materials such as steel, gold and coral.*

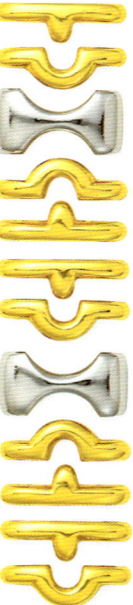

166. *Five gold* Parentesi *necklaces showing how the modular elements, featured above, can be made more or less precious by encrusting them with diamonds or substituting them with semiprecious gemstones or steel. From top left: gold combined with cabochon sapphires and diamonds; all gold; all gold; gold and diamonds; gold and carved amethysts, citrines, blue topazes, green tourmalines. Thanks to their versatility and wearability,* Parentesi *jewels, first created in 1982, have been successful and widely copied.*

THE POWER OF BVLGARI DESIGN

carved coral, mother-of-pearl, or semiprecious stones (ill. 163-166). The *Parentesi* module can also be adapted in length and extended to incorporate a coloured cabochon gemstone or an antique coin in the connecting element either (ill. 166).

Furthermore, gold *Parentesi* elements can be constructed in such a way as to allow them to slide on flattened *Tubo gas* steel bands. Sometimes the *Parentesi* is rotated 90 degrees in order to form a gold chain which in turn can be graduated in size. In addition, this module format is advantageous in that it can be readily adapted to different size wrists and necks by the simple addition or removal of one or more elements.

The *Parentesi* module provides high quality of design and high quality of manufacture at a wide price range – from steel and gold rings to diamond encrusted parures. This was the perfect answer for women of the 1980's who required stylish and wearable jewels to replace conventional – and now obsolete – formal high jewellery. Grand occasions such as elegant balls and opera premieres had ceased to be the setting for the display of lavish jewellery mounted with large gemstones in white metal. Women established in the world of business required jewels that suited their working lifestyle – from a board meeting to a cocktail party – jewels that could be worn from morning to night. Jewels that "a woman can wear [...] to a ball or to a picnic," as Nicola Bulgari said (*Vogue*, USA, October 1995).

Bulgari *Parentesi* jewels provided the ideal answer by being wearable, decorative, bold and suitable for these and other occasions. Moreover, since the *Parentesi* module was immediately recognisable as Bulgari's, it provided a sought after status symbol much like a designer accessory.

As mentioned above, the *Parentesi* module has been one of the most extensively copied designs of the last two decades. The imitations, however, have never achieved the same standard of excellence. When compared to Bulgari *Parentesi*, such copies generally display a poor rendering of proportions and quality of workmanship. They are also either too heavy or too light – never of the "right" weight, a feature of all Bulgari creations.

167. *Two gold and diamond* Trika *bracelet-watches (1995). The name* Trika *– Greek for braid – is given to this model due to its intricate braided pattern. Its extreme flexibility is a novel feature in the production of Bulgari jewelled bracelet-watches and is a departure from the earlier rigid bangle-watches. Each bracelet is formed by 187 parts cast from 35 different moulds.*

From the "Doppio Cuore" to the "Trika"

The unforeseen and extraordinary success of the *Parentesi* prompted Bulgari to apply the same module concept to other motifs. The most prominent feature of modular jewels, made up of the same elements, is that they come to form a "family," that is to say a recognisable line of jewels. From 1982 on, the "module" concept has been skilfully developed by the Bulgari team of designers to include: the *Doppio Cuore* (double heart) of 1983; the *Boules* (beads) of 1986; the *Gancio* (hook) of 1987; the *Alveare* of 1988, reminiscent of the structure of a beehive; the *Saetta* (thunderbolt) of 1990, reminiscent of the one held by Zeus; the *Spiga* (ear of wheat) of 1990; the *Celtica*, of 1993, inspired by bronze Celtic bracelets or anklets of the 3rd century BC; *Doppio Passo* (inspired by classical ballet) of 1993; and *Trika* ("braid" in Greek) of 1996 (ill. 127, 167-174).

168. *The Alveare modular line of 1988 followed in the wake of the success of the* Parentesi. *Characteristically, the honeycomb modules can be assembled to create a variety of jewels ranging from necklaces to rings.*

BVLGARI

The *Gancio* (ill. 171) and *Boules* modules, formed by rounded, three-dimensional motifs, differ from the flatter and more two-dimensional rendering of the other modules. In particular, their design permits the inclusion of rounded elements in the assemblage: examples include pearls, hard stone beads and faceted roundels of semiprecious coloured gemstones.

Bulgari modules are characteristically fashioned by simple yet effective forms, reproduced in series, which interlock and do not require any additional decoration. With the employment of the modular concept, Bulgari has perfected, in the 20th century, a long-standing aspiration shared by jewellers since Antiquity. In ancient times, Hellenistic craftsmen were the first to realise the benefits of reproducing in series; they created rosettes and amphorae motifs which they then assembled either as necklaces, earrings or hair ornaments. The concept was similarly exploited by Castellani in the 19th century with his disc and floret motifs. Later, in the 1940s, Trabert and Hoeffer, Mauboussin followed suit with their line of gold jewels called "Reflection: Your Personality".

In conclusion, the success of the Bulgari jewels results from bold, carefully conceived designs, coupled with versatility and a wide price range. They are jewels of modern, uncluttered simplicity wearable with everything from jeans to ballgowns. Bulgari's achievements are reached through a laborious and lengthy process of selection of designs and prototypes. These points are frequently made by Paolo Bulgari, who says: "*È più difficile fare un bel gioiello da dieci milioni che uno da un miliardo*" – "It is more difficult to create an attractive jewel worth ten million lira than one worth a billion."

169. *Five images illustrating the production of* Alveare *jewels which entail skilled manual labour. Though each single modular element is cast and produced in series, it is always finished by hand. The hand finishing process accounts for up to fifty percent of the total manufacturing time.*

THE POWER OF BVLGARI DESIGN

170. *A selection of Alveare jewels including a necklace, two bangles and two rings. In these examples steel and diamonds are used in order to vary the Alveare original plain gold pattern.*

171. *A group of gold and variously set modular jewels including: three pairs of* Doppio Cuore *earclips and a* Doppio Cuore *ring; two pairs of* Gancio *earclips; a pair of* Saetta *earclips.*

THE POWER OF BVLGARI DESIGN

172. *A selection of Spiga jewels in white and yellow gold. The two necklaces and the bracelet are embellished with brilliant-cut diamonds, the ring is in plain gold. This design was created in 1990, yet another successful application of the modular principle.*

BVLGARI

173. *A range of colourful modular necklaces realised in a variety of materials including gold, steel, semiprecious gemstones, cultured pearls, diamonds and porcelain. On the left, from top to bottom:*

SILVER AND PRECIOUS OBJECTS

Doppio Cuore *(1983)*, Boules *(1986)*, Boules *(1986)*, Gancio *(1987)*; Gancio *(1987)*.
On the right, from top to bottom: Gancio *(1987)*, Gancio *(1987)*, Saetta *(1990)*, Doppio Passo *(1993)*, Chandra *(1994)*.

149

THE TUBOGAS

The warm, solar colour of yellow gold and its malleability have been employed extensively by Bulgari since the 1970s, and to great effect. Yellow gold is undoubtedly one of the firm's trademarks. The reason Bulgari has favoured the use of gold is that, unlike other precious metals, the warm hue of yellow gold allows even extremely important gems to be worn in a casual manner. In other words, by combining yellow gold with an important diamond, a "demystification" occurs: the precious gem, while still retaining its beauty and value, becomes instantly more wearable.

One of Bulgari's tenets is that jewels should not be relegated to a safe but should be part of everyday life and suited for all occasions. Nicola Bulgari said: "All of it is meant to be worn – not to be kept in a safe deposit box. The jewels compliment and are an addition to what the person is wearing... They are made to be worn from morning to evening... Some women do not take them off to go to bed" (*The Middlesex News*, 12 August 1982). It is therefore not surprising that the firm has favoured the use of yellow gold above all other precious metals. Yellow gold at Bulgari is used for a great variety of purposes, ranging from jewels to objects, from the settings of precious gems to the mountings of semiprecious stones, from chains to evening bags. Regardless of the different forms, shapes and functions, Bulgari's gold is always polished and worked into forms characterised by smooth contours. One of the most characteristic and successful renderings is the gold *Tubogas*: a flexible band of sleek and polished contours produced without soldering (ill. 179). Its construction, which requires hours of skilled craftsmanship, consists of wrapping two long gold strips with raised edges around a core – either of copper or wood. The edges then interlock onto one another, requiring no soldering. The

174. *Advertisement, 1994, from the* Metamorphosis *campaign started in 1992.*

BVLGARI

THE TUBOGAS

175. *A selection of Tubogas jewels of the 1980s and early 1990s. These are designed as flexible bands made of two long strips of metal with raised edges which interlock into one another, requiring no soldering. One of the bracelets is designed as a triple coil of pink, yellow and white gold; the other is set with a heart-shaped tourmaline. Necklaces, as the illustrated examples, can be formed by either single or multiple rows of gold Tubogas. Note the sliding clasp, a feature which enables adjustment and perfect fit around the wearer's neck.*

153

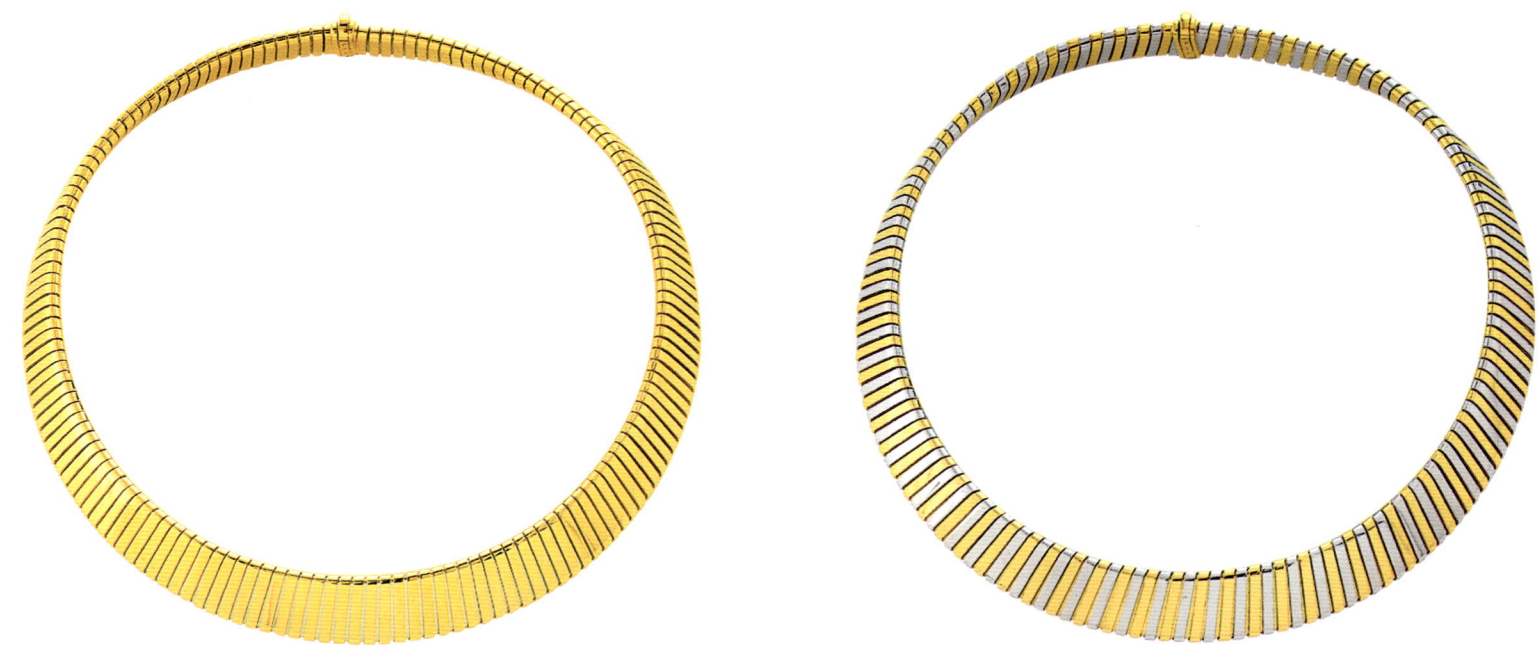
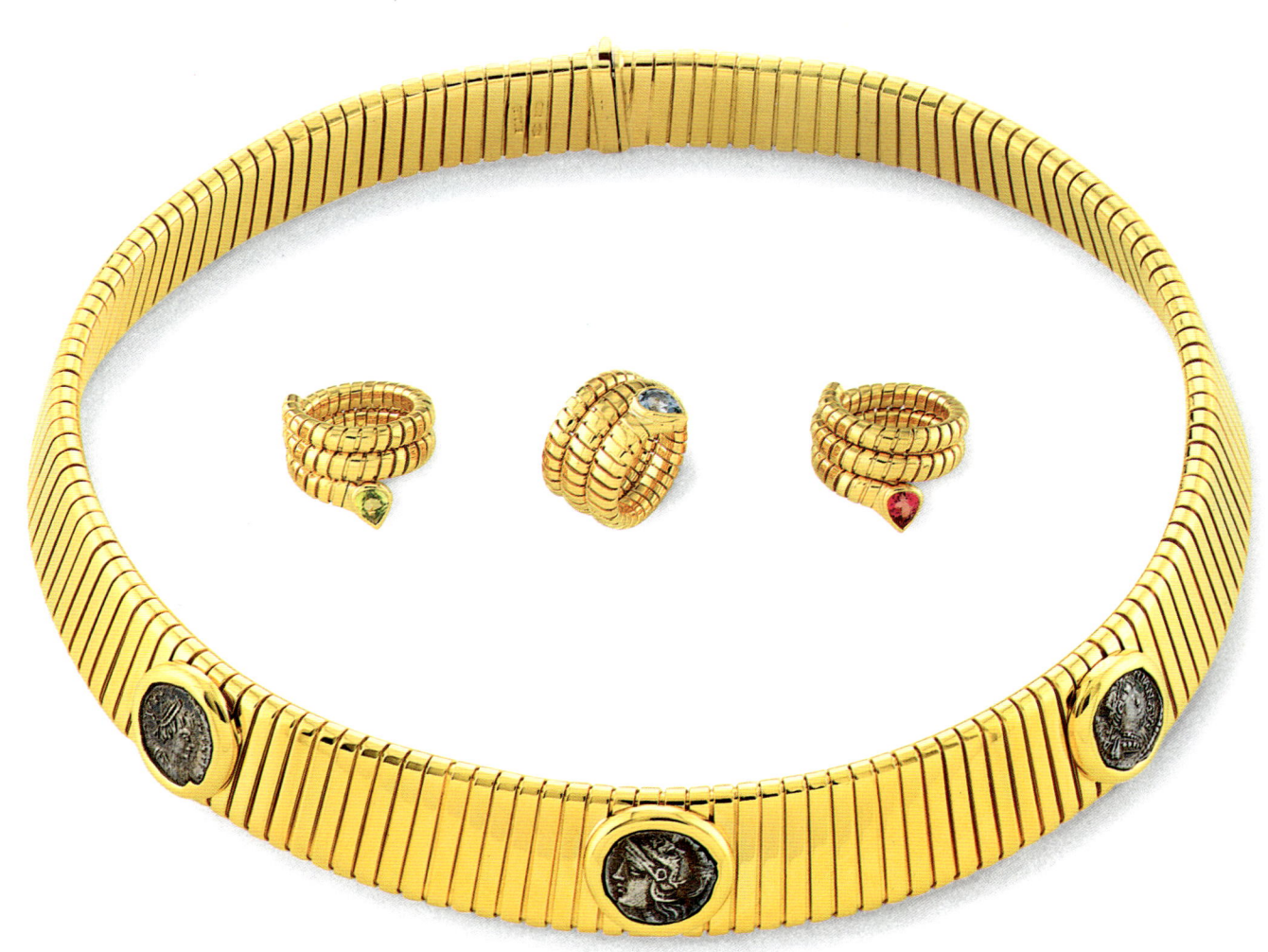

176. *A selection of* Tubogas *jewels of the 1990s. One of the necklaces is designed as a simple yellow gold band; the second is made of gold bands of contrasting colours – yellow and white; the third, in yellow gold, is set at the front with three ancient bronze coins. The three rings are designed as triple coils and are set with pear-shaped coloured gemstones.*

177. *The coiled* Tubogas *bracelet-watch of stylised serpent design has become one of the firm's trademarks. The yellow gold example with drop-shaped face dates from the early 1980s.*

core is then removed, either by simply drawing it out or dissolving it in acid. The flexibility of such a gold band is truly remarkable and has been employed to great effect in the production of necklaces formed by single or multiple bands of *Tubogas* (ill. 175, 176). The most impressive of these necklaces consist of four or five bands placed one above the other. The final creations are spectacular collars which encase the neck and are often decorated at the front with coins or gems. In addition to necklaces, rings, bracelets and watches are also formed by *Tubogas* bands, at times arranged in multiple coils (ill. 175-177). In particular, the coiled *Tubogas* bracelet-watch of stylised serpent design has become one of the firm's trademarks (ill. 177). A symbol of knowledge and eternity, serpents have wound their way through the history of jewellery design from Hellenistic times to the present. Bulgari, always conscious of its ancient cultural heritage, has drawn from this tradition. The firm's snake jewels are a reinterpretation of the past, yet the results are very much of today and even of tomorrow.

178. *Two gold* BVLGARI-BVLGARI *watches mounted on Tubogas bands. One is designed as a triple coil of yellow, pink and white gold. The other consists of a single band of yellow gold.*

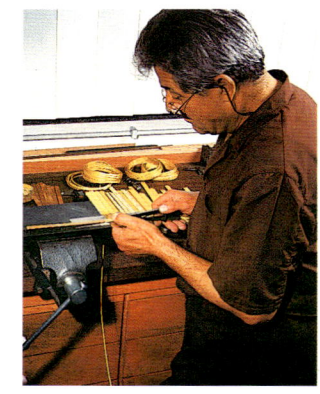

THE TUBOGAS

The play of metals of contrasting colours is another characteristic ingredient of Bulgari jewels. This feature is particularly evident in jewels mounted with ancient coins (ill. 154) as well as in *Tubogas* jewels formed by yellow, pink and white gold (ill. 178).

The desire to maximise the use of metals of contrasting colours brought Bulgari, in the late 1970s, also to use grey steel in combination with yellow gold. This involved a lengthy process of technological research which led Bulgari to select a type of steel which for its properties is normally employed in diverse spheres such as motor, aeronautical, naval, chemical and medical industries.

This particular type of steel was deemed suitable in colour – complementing the warm hues of red and yellow gold; it is absolutely stainless and suitable for microfusion. The problems that Bulgari had to face and solve in the working of steel were related to its high melting point (1300-1500 °C) and its low malleability, compared to 18-carat gold. The working of *Tubogas* in steel is much more labour intensive than that of *Tubogas* in gold. Thus steel, while cheaper, costs more to process: working 10 cm of steel *Tubogas* costs 10% more than working the same length of gold.

Bulgari's unconventional approach to jewellery is thus confirmed. Just as the firm has dared to juxtapose the finest and most costly gems with much less precious stones – for sake of colour effect – it has also combined the magic of gold with the utilitarian quality of steel in order to achieve a striking ornament.

179. *The sequence shows different stages of the manufacture of* Tubogas *jewels. The process requires hours of skilled craftsmanship and consists of wrapping two long gold strips, in some cases of contrasting colour, around a core – of either copper or wood. The gold strips have raised edges which interlock into one another, requiring no soldering. The core is subsequently removed, by either simply drawing it out or dissolving it in acid. The flexible band is then shaped into necklaces, bracelets, rings and bracelet-watches, which fit perfectly and very comfortably around neck, arm or finger.*

A Unique Sense of Volume

Volume of a jewel is a constant concern at Bulgari. All the firm's jewels have a three-dimensional quality which is unmistakable. For Bulgari, a jewel is never a mere transposition in stone and precious metal of the original two-dimensional design, but rather a creation which takes form in space, breathing a life of its own. This process can be equated with an architectural plan initially drawn on paper in two dimensions and then translated into the three-dimensional structure of the finished building.

This three-dimensional effect is often achieved at Bulgari by means of a bombé or convex front, often backed by a lattice framework, a feature best illustrated in jewels such as the gold and diamond necklace of interlaced motifs on pages 161-162. Here the pronounced rounded front is echoed by a similarly patterned reverse. This conveys not only the idea of volume but also of substance. At times instead it is the play between juxtaposed convex and concave elements which enforces the sense of volume (ill. 181). In addition, volume in most Bulgari designs is enhanced by the extensive use of rounded decorative elements and smooth outlines, further reinforced by the frequent use of cabochon gemstones. These project above their collet settings conveying a sense of volume and space, like cupolas above their drums (ill. 186, 187). It is not surprising that Bulgari tries to match in miniature the concept of the cupola – the architectural form which marks the apogee of Roman architecture. Since Mycenean times architects had been striving to develop dome-shaped structures such as the Tholos (1500-1225 BC); however it was only at the time of the Romans that true free standing domes were erected successfully. Among these undoubtedly the most outstanding and monumental is the Pantheon in Rome completed under the Emperor Hadrian

180. *Advertisement, 1976.*

BVLGARI

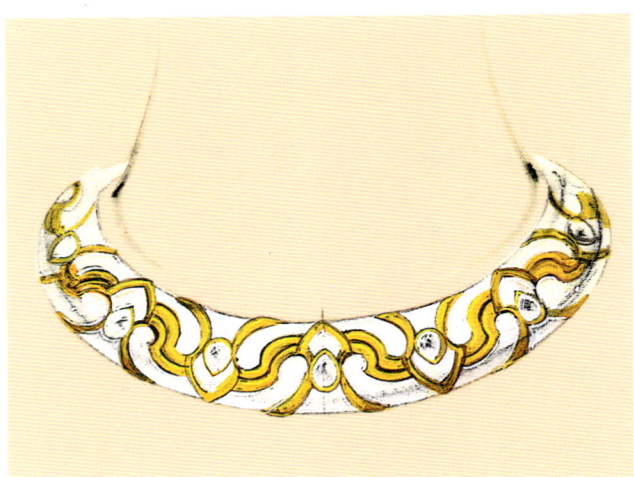

182. Design for the necklace illustrated below. Note how even in the two-dimensional drawing, volume is emphasised.

181. A gold and diamond necklace pavé-set with 33.82 carats of brilliant-cut diamonds and 16 larger pear-shaped stones for a total weight of 15.37 carats (1990). Characteristically, the necklace is not conceived as a flat band but as a convex ornament backed by an intricate gold trellis work. The decoration is also articulated on different planes: one for the pavé of diamonds, one for the gold strap-work, and one for the large pear-shaped diamonds.

A UNIQUE SENSE OF VOLUME

183. *A gold and diamond collar (1995), pavé-set with 62.73 carats of brilliant-cut diamonds, part of the Bulgari Collection Internationale. The jewel is typical of Bulgari in its rounded contours, substantial volume and beautifully crafted open-work reverse. The pattern and design of the reverse (illustrated on page 162) are so fine that one might consider wearing the necklace inside-out. The total weight of 308.36 grams is substantial, but at the same time pleasing and comfortable to wear. Bulgari always strives to achieve the "ideal" weight for a jewel.*

161

184. *Reverse of the gold and diamond necklace illustrated on the previous page.*

A UNIQUE SENSE OF VOLUME

(AD 117-138). This explains how the choice of the cupola element in Bulgari may be seen not only as fulfilling requirements for volume but also as yet another reference to the firm's Greek and Roman cultural heritage. This in turn explains why Bulgari was among the first to reinstate fine cabochon gemstones in high jewellery. Rounded polished cabochon rather than faceted gemstones had been used in antiquity and during the Renaissance, mainly because lapidary techniques were not particularly sophisticated at the time (it was easier to polish rather than facet). Later, when the art of faceting gemstones had improved, all fine gemstones would be faceted. Only those of lower intrinsic value would be left *en cabochon*, for example the "carbuncle" or almandine garnets in 19th-century jewellery. By the beginning of the 20th century this state of affairs had changed, and in jewels of the 1920s one finds a prolific use both of fine and

185. *Detail of a gold and diamond necklace (1995). The diamond-set bell-shaped drops are arranged in three tiers. A moment of the manufacturing process is pictured above and shows how each element is secured separately to the frame, allowing extreme flexibility.*

186. *A ring set with a cabochon sapphire of 122.13 carats within a diamond border, and a ring decorated with a Colombian cabochon emerald in a domed setting of diamonds and emeralds.*

187. *A selection of gem-set rings created by Bulgari from approximately 1975 to 1995. From top to bottom: a cabochon sapphire from Burma, of 14.13 carats, in a brick-work pattern diamond-set mount; a cabochon sapphire from Burma in a domed mount, the shoulders enhanced by calibré-cut emeralds which guide the eye to the central gem; a superb Colombian cabochon emerald ring, the fine gem projecting from a double row of square-cut diamonds like a cupola from its drum; a ring with a Colombian cabochon emerald set in a ruby and diamond domed mount.*

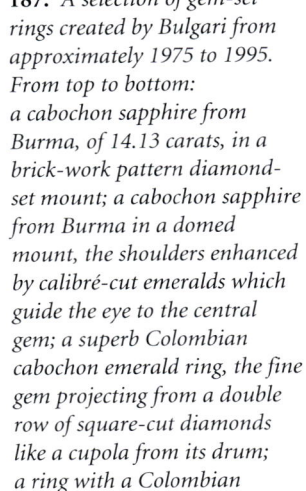

A UNIQUE SENSE OF VOLUME

188. *Five* Tronchetto *rings (1990-95) respectively set with pink tourmaline, peridot, red tourmaline, iolite, garnet. The gems have been fashioned with a cabochon top. Their rounded surface prevents them from being chipped by wear.*

semiprecious gemstones *en cabochon*. These stones, however, were shaped in this fashion not only to provide volume but also contrast between the translucent effect of the cabochon coloured stone and the glittering sparkle of the faceted diamonds.

By the 1940s the use of cabochon gemstones, both precious and semiprecious, had subsided, and this remained so during the following decades. In the 1950s, faceted gemstones mounted in claw settings prevailed in jewellery and similarly in the 1960s, where one finds both faceted gems and uncut gemstones but hardly ever cabochons. It was largely thanks to Bulgari that in the late 1960s the cabochon way of fashioning gemstones, both for precious and semiprecious gems, was finally reintroduced (ill. 101-108).

Since then Bulgari has made extensive use of cabochon stones: these range from exceptionally fine quality emeralds and sapphires (ill. 204, 207) to more modest and decorative semiprecious stones such as amethysts and citrines (ill. 203). As always, these cabochons successfully render the volume or "cupola" effect of the jewel, which is further enhanced by their setting. These are never spiky claws but rounded and smooth collets which enhance the overall rounded

189. *Four gold* Doppio Baccellato *(reeded) rings set with cabochon gems: iolite and peridot, blue topaz and amethyst, amethyst and citrine quartz, peridot and amethyst.*

165

shapes of the design. Often the cupola effect is also emphasised by building a domed structure around the cabochon stone, which is then decorated with gems in pavé-settings treated just as slates or tiles on a domed roof. A fine example of this style of setting is given by the cabochon Burmese sapphire ring illustrated on page 164 (ill. 187).

Finally, the use of cabochon gemstones conveys a sense of volume also to linear and mainly two-dimensional structures such as those of filed curb-linking chains, which may be seen in the illustrated examples (ill. 190).

The Ideal Weight

At Bulgari volume in a jewel is always combined with substantial weight. Fine and well constructed ornaments should never be too flimsy or too light nor should they be too heavy and cumbersome, but they should always present a certain weight. This feature is noticeable in most of Bulgari's jewels and goes hand in hand with its concern for volume.

Bulgari always strives to create the ideal weight in a jewel. In the case of Bulgari necklaces the wearers will always be pleasantly aware of these ornaments at the base of their neck. "They are weighted to fit on a woman's neck just exactly right... It is a painstaking work," says Nicola Bulgari. Their weight is never uncomfortable but, to the contrary, generates pleasure: a pleasure in the awareness of the weight and substance of the precious materials forming the ornament.

Fine jewels should look good, but also feel good, when worn. When this combination occurs, one is instinctively drawn to caress one's jewels deriving pleasure from this tactile experience. This characteristic is a feature of Bulgari's jewellery, which is always very pleasing to wear and touch.

Wearability is one of the firm's main concerns: this has been confirmed by Paolo Bulgari, who said that his aim is to create "jewellery [...] which any woman would want to wear all day long." At Bulgari a lot of time is spent experimenting with numerous samples of jewels in order to achieve the ideal weight and wearability which harmonise with the body.

A UNIQUE SENSE OF VOLUME

190. *Two gold necklaces of filed curb linking (circa 1980) set respectively with cabochon sapphires alternating with cabochon rubies, and with pink corals, pink and green tourmalines, quartzes and amethysts.*

Colour and Fabulous Gemstones

Diamonds

Bulgari has always been concerned with the quality and beauty of the gems mounted in its creations. Since the early post-war years, the firm has distinguished itself among Italian jewellers by using the finest diamonds and coloured gems – rubies from Burma, emeralds from Colombia and sapphires from Kashmir. These were carefully selected for the beauty of their colours and care was taken to avoid unseemly inclusions. Giorgio and his sons have combed the international gem markets relentlessly in their quest for perfect gems.

Though colour might be considered the dominant feature of most of Bulgari's jewels, a number of colourless diamonds of exceptional size, whiteness, cut and clarity have also been mounted by the firm. In keeping with its reputation of fine jewellers, Bulgari has traded some of the rarest and most historically important diamonds as they came onto the market this century. Among the numerous examples is the "Nassak" diamond. This famous stone, originally 89 carats and 2 grains, was named after the Indian city of Nasik, situated north-east of Bombay. Here it served, probably from the 17th century on, as the eye of a statue of the Hindu god Siva. In the early 19th century it was brought to Britain and, in 1837, it was acquired by the first Marquis of Westminster who used it to decorate the hilt of his sword. Subsequently it was re-cut to its present size of 43.38 carats and thereafter changed hands a number of times. In 1970 it was offered at public auction in New York, where it fetched a then record price of 500,000 dollars. Shortly afterwards, it was acquired jointly by Bulgari and the Boston firm of J. & S.S. In 1977 Bulgari and J. & S.S. offered it to the King of Saudi Arabia who had been captivated both by its beauty (D colour - Flawless) and its fascinating history. The king

191. *Advertisement, 1960-65.*

192. *An exceptional fancy lilac pink step-cut diamond weighing 24.44 carats. This stone, originally purchased by Count Vittorio Cini at Bulgari, was bought back by the firm years later and sold to a prominent collector in the 1950s. The gem was lost in a Rome nightclub and resurfaced at public auction in 1976 where it fetched the then record price of 2,700,000 Swiss francs against a pre-sale estimate of 1,200,000-1,400,000.*

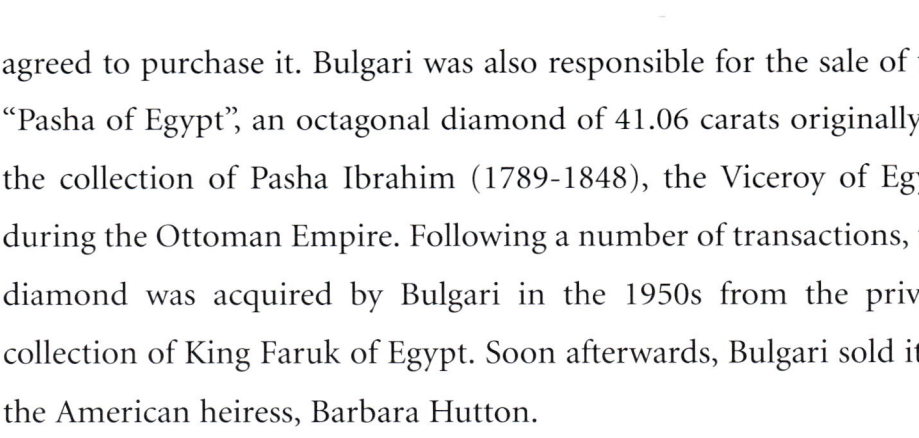

194. *A fine emerald and diamond necklace (1960s), set at the front with seven circular Colombian emeralds within borders of marquise and brilliant-cut diamonds. An example of lavish use of exceptional quality gemstones.*

193. *Although Bulgari is best known for mounting important coloured gemstones and diamonds in yellow gold, white gold and platinum have been frequently used by the firm to underscore the whiteness of high-quality diamonds. A good example is the diamond engagement ring of model Claudia Schiffer (1994) illustrated here. The oval diamond of 4.72 carats is simply set between tapered baguette diamond shoulders. The platinum shank is inscribed: "D ♥ C for ever".*

195. *Two gem-set rings of the 1980s formerly in the collection of pop star Elton John. The fine square step-cut emerald weighs 4.36 carats and the octagonal step-cut diamond weighs 4.33 carats. Typically, in both cases the central gemstone is mounted in a smooth collet rather than claws. The diamond ring illustrates how Bulgari favours the use of yellow gold and coloured gemstone surrounds.*

agreed to purchase it. Bulgari was also responsible for the sale of the "Pasha of Egypt", an octagonal diamond of 41.06 carats originally in the collection of Pasha Ibrahim (1789-1848), the Viceroy of Egypt during the Ottoman Empire. Following a number of transactions, the diamond was acquired by Bulgari in the 1950s from the private collection of King Faruk of Egypt. Soon afterwards, Bulgari sold it to the American heiress, Barbara Hutton.

Besides securing deals involving gemstones of extraordinary value, Bulgari has also been witness over the years to unusual stories involving precious gems. One of the most sensational episodes occurred in 1977 at Bulgari New York. A guest at the Pierre Hotel called the shop requesting that a salesperson be sent up to his suite with a selection of rings. When the salesman returned, one of the diamond rings worth 35,000 dollars was missing. It was a rather large

COLOUR AND FABULOUS GEMSTONES

196. *A fine gem-set necklace of 1994, mounted with 233.04 carats of pale blue, yellow and pink sapphires and with 23 cultured pearls tipped with cabochon rubies. The choice of a pale palette is typical of the 1990s and differs from earlier examples usually mounted with gemstones of more vivid and contrasting colours.*

197. *This spectacular ruby and diamond necklace from the* Bulgari Collection Internationale *was created in 1994 and is set with 48 rubies of exceptional quality, weighing a total of 59.33 carats, and baguette and brilliant-cut diamonds – weighing 13.94 carats. This necklace was worn, together with a pair of matching earrings, by Sophia Loren in the film* Prêt-à-Porter, *in the scene of the launch of the* Chandra *collection. The beautiful pattern of the reverse of the mount and the detail of the front illustrate two typical features of Bulgari: perfect craftsmanship and perfect match in colour and size of the stones.*

COLOUR AND FABULOUS GEMSTONES

198. *An emerald and diamond necklace from the Bulgari Collection Internationale (1993). The seven exceptionally fine Colombian cabochon emeralds weigh a total of 46.58 carats and are perfectly matched in colour and shape. They are offset by a pavé of baguette and brilliant-cut diamonds for a total weight of 31.38 carats. This is a good example of how Bulgari chooses to fashion even the finest gems en cabochon.*

199. *A fine pair of emerald and diamond pendant earclips of 1993, en suite with the necklace illustrated on the previous page. The four Colombian cabochon emeralds weigh a total of 15.80 carats. The reverse shows the characteristic griglia (grid-like backing) inscribed with the weights of the individual gems, and the signature "BVLGARI".*

200. *A pair of diamond and emerald earclips and another pair of emerald, ruby and diamond earclips (late 1980s). In the first case, note how the buff-top cabochon emeralds have been used to underscore the larger heart-shaped diamonds. In the second case, Bulgari relies on one of its favourite colour combinations: red, green and white.*

ring set with two emerald-cut diamonds for a total of 4 carats. Soon after, the man, a notorious swindler, managed to check out from the hotel. A year later, however, he was arrested for unrelated fraud charges and died in a Michigan jail. During a routine autopsy, doctors found the missing ring in the man's stomach.

Not only exceptional white diamonds but also rare and extremely precious coloured diamonds – known as "fancy diamonds" – have been mounted by Bulgari. These range from pink to blue, from yellow to green and from lilac to purple. In the late 1950s, the firm purchased an extraordinarily fine and large collection of fancy coloured diamonds of the most diverse colours and shapes. They had been the pride of a well-known French diamond dealer who had assembled hundreds of carats of fancy diamonds over many years. When they reached Bulgari, the diamonds were mounted in a variety of jewels. Amongst the most effective designs were a series of brooches of floral

COLOUR AND FABULOUS GEMSTONES

201. *Another necklace from the* Bulgari Collection Internationale *(1994). In this case the scalloped collar, entirely pavé-set with baguette and brilliant-cut diamonds, is mounted with 70.07 carats of sapphires, beautifully matched in colour, and 6.17 carats of larger pear-shaped diamonds.*

COLOUR AND FABULOUS GEMSTONES

202. *Reverse and detail of the sapphire and diamond necklace illustrated on the previous page. In order to offer the ultimate service to its clientele the firm created, in 1996, the "Bulgari Gemmological Centre". This department provides gemmological certifications for most major gemstones mounted by the firm.*

inspiration. The petals were realistically suggested by the use of the coloured diamonds mounted in delicate tremblant settings, permitting the stones to flicker at every movement like a flower caught in a breeze (ill. 93-95, 99).

Many coloured diamonds of substantial weight have been handled by Bulgari. Among the most exceptional are a 10 carat pear-shaped pink diamond sold to Imelda Marcos and a superb 24.44 carat step-cut lilac pink diamond (ill. 192) which was originally purchased by Giorgio Bulgari in the 1930s and sold to one of the firm's most important clients of the day, the Venetian Count Vittorio Cini. At a later date, it was re-purchased by Bulgari, who in the 1950s sold it to an Italian industrialist who gave it as a wedding gift to his future wife. In 1970, however, the recipient of this magnificent diamond lost the stone in a nightclub off the Via Veneto in Rome. The gem was found at 4 a.m. by one of the club's cabaret dancers after work. Not realising the extraordinary value of the stone, the dancer gave it to his mother as a gift. Though regarding it as a nearly worthless bauble, she became very attached to the jewel and at her death even contemplated having it buried with her. In the event, however, the gem was appraised and found to be of great worth. As the stone had never been claimed, the son was advised to consign it for auction. It was offered for sale at Sotheby's Zurich in 1976, where it fetched a record price at the time of 2,700,000 Swiss francs. The stone was purchased at the sale by a renowned international gems dealer and is now reported to be in the collection of the Royal Family of Saudi Arabia.

Coloured Gems

Apart from mounting diamonds, Bulgari is renown for setting large gem-quality coloured stones – rubies, sapphires and emeralds. These tend to be fashioned *en cabochon*, simply mounted in claws or collets and enhanced only by a few diamonds to add sparkle to the richness and intensity of their colour. Traditionally the cabochon cut, which consists of polishing rather than faceting the gem, had been confined to gemstones of mediocre clarity. This enabled lapidaries to exploit the colour of the stone while limiting the

203. *Four gem-set necklaces from the* Bulgari Collection Internationale. *These jewels epitomise the Bulgari style of the late 1980s and early 1990s. They are characterised by volume, rounded outlines and unusual and bold colour combinations, where exceptionally fine gemstones such as emeralds, rubies and diamonds are juxtaposed with gems of much lower intrinsic value such as amethysts and citrines. Apart from one example, the cuts of the larger stones are characteristically cabochon rather than faceted, and the smaller stones are calibrated to fit the curves of the mounts.*

COLOUR AND FABULOUS GEMSTONES

BVLGARI

204. *A magnificent necklace from the 1990 Bulgari Collection Internationale, a fine and representative example of a carefully planned arrangement of gemstones according to the harmony of colour. The striking central juxtaposition of green and red is then attenuated by the purple of the amethysts at the sides. Typically, Bulgari does not refrain from combining a rare and precious heart-shaped cabochon emerald with less costly amethysts in order to achieve the perfect "harmony of colours." Details of this fine jewel are illustrated at the bottom of the page.*

display of flaws and inclusions. Bulgari, however, was amongst the first jewellers in the second half of the 20th century to maximise the potential of the cabochon cut, applying it as never before to gems of outstanding clarity. The use of fine and rare gems cut *en cabochon* has been and still is one of the firm's most recognisable traits. The 1993 necklace set with seven cabochon emeralds totalling 46.58 carats and the 1989 ring set with a Burmese sugar-loaf cabochon (a cabochon with ribbed sides) of 14.13 carats are magnificent examples of how Bulgari has used this cut for exceptionally fine gems (ill. 187, 198). The firm is also known for having handled historically important coloured gemstones, such as carved emeralds and ruby beads from the fabled collection of Nizams of Hyderabad, Muslim rulers of great wealth, whose authority once extended across much of southern India (ill. 116).

  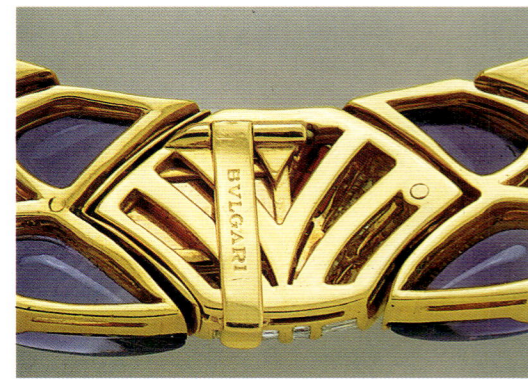

Harmony of Colours

Since its beginning, the firm has favoured the use of coloured stones over diamonds; therefore, it is not surprising that one of Bulgari's greatest achievements lies in successfully overturning the long-standing traditional hierarchy of gemstones in high jewellery.

For decades the triad – ruby, emerald and sapphire – had been used exclusively in combination with diamonds. This conventional approach resulted inevitably in a rather predictable and limited range of colour combinations where the vibrant red, green and blue were offset only by the white diamonds.

In order to overcome this monotony, Bulgari, especially from the mid-1960s on, began to revolutionise jewellery design with an innovative and daring process. Initially it started combining rubies, sapphires and emeralds not only with diamonds, but also among themselves in bold combinations of colours such as red, green and white (ruby, emerald and diamonds) or red, blue and white (ruby, sapphire and diamonds) (ill. 106-110). Gradually, however, Bulgari also began combining rubies, emeralds and sapphires with less precious but equally beautiful gemstones, such as amethysts, citrines, tourmalines, coral, pearls and garnets. This led to a still wider range of colours, including new and underutilised shades of violets, pinks, deep reds, greens and yellows. The result has been an almost endless choice of chromatic combinations ranging from bold juxtapositions of primary colours to more subtle combinations of graduated hues (ill. 203).

The bold and striking colour combinations for which Bulgari is now so renowned are not the result of haphazard juxtaposition of gemstones; on the contrary, they are the culmination of a lengthy process of thought and design. Just as a composer, when writing his music, works out the rules of harmony and rhythm based on firm mathematical principles, similarly Bulgari assembles and combines variously coloured gems according to precise rules. It is the harmony of colour rather than the intrinsic value of the gems that is at the core of all Bulgari creations. Given an imaginary circular display of the colour spectrum of light, it has been proven that subtle and subdued effects may be obtained by combining consecutive colours on the

COLOUR AND FABULOUS GEMSTONES

205. *Colour is of paramount importance for Bulgari, as seen in the Carré line of jewels (1987), reminiscent of patterns of formal gardens or floor mosaics. This selection of brooches and designs shows how the same pattern can be altered time and again by infinite colour combinations. Typically, precious and semiprecious stones are calibrated to fit the shape of the mount. The three Carré brooches illustrated here – one set in 1990 with a gold stater of Philip II of Macedonia (359-336 BC), one set with a large natural pearl of 40.02 grains in 1990 – are both in surrounds of calibrated rubies and amethysts. The third (1988) is decorated with a checkerboard of blue topazes, amethysts, peridots, pink and red tourmalines.*

183

spectrum such as violet, blue and green; the most powerful and striking impact, however, may be obtained by juxtaposing colours situated at opposite sides of the spectrum, such as violet and yellow, or green and red.

An example of this arrangement of gemstones is shown by a magnificent emerald, ruby, diamond and amethyst necklace created in 1990 (ill. 204). The focus of the jewel is its centre: a fine cabochon emerald of 36.07 carats offset by a contour of rubies. It is not a coincidence that Bulgari chose red for the green emerald surround, for it is its intent to maximise the impact of the large gem and to draw the eye to the centre of the jewel. In this instance the effect is achieved by combining red and green, colours situated at opposite ends of the spectrum.

The impact of the juxtaposition is attenuated, however, by the

206. *A group of* Naturalia *jewels and designs. This line, a celebration of nature in stylised forms, is characterised by the use of coloured precious and semiprecious gemstones carved in different and unusual shapes, often offset by diamonds. The stylised fish motif is perhaps the most successful of the range and is the final result of a lengthy process of design. The earclips (1991) are formed by a large fish surmount supporting three small fish drops in a pattern known as* Mamma Pesce *(Mother Fish). The fish pattern is also repeated on the bracelet (1991), set with coral, chalcedony, amethyst citrines, tourmalines and diamonds.*

restrained use of red and by the fact that it blends with the violet of the amethyst on the side – red and violet being consecutive colours. Overall, thanks to this careful arrangement, the jewel is a balanced object with a central accent attenuated on the sides. The diamonds merely play a complementary role, providing sparkle.

Thus, Bulgari's choice and juxtaposition of gemstones is unusual, daring and their combinations are dictated exclusively by aesthetic reasons. The traditional principle of using gemstones based exclusively on their intrinsic value is subordinated to an appreciation of their aesthetic qualities. In Bulgari jewellery, gemstones are used mainly for their colour potential, often without regard for their intrinsic worth. When the two aspects happen to coincide, this is considered a fortuitous coincidence. This is true not only of the more decorative and less precious creations, but also of the unique jewels of the *Bulgari Collection Internationale* – a collection of costly, one-off jewellery, which is displayed on rotation throughout Bulgari outlets worldwide. In this collection the finest and rarest gemstones are often combined with stones of relatively low intrinsic value, which are chosen only for their appealing colours.

It is not unusual to find in these creations relatively inexpensive amethysts combined with the finest emeralds, or pale sapphires combined with the rarest Burmese rubies. For at Bulgari it is the inherent beauty of the jewel conceived as a work of art that comes before the intrinsic value of its materials.

In a Bulgari jewel, the cut of a given stone is also of prime importance. Frequently one finds the conventional cuts: brilliants, marquises, pear-shaped and step-cuts for diamonds, cushions for sapphires and rubies, and step-cuts for emeralds. One also finds, however, a large number of cabochons, heart-shaped stones and unusual calibrated gems known in the trade as "calibré-cut" stones, specifically shaped to fit a given mount. It is not a coincidence that this latter type of cut had not been used extensively in high jewellery since the 1920s as it is very labour intensive, and therefore costly, manner of fashioning stones. Bulgari revived the use of calibré-cut stones in the 1970s (ill. 114). Each small stone that the firm uses is individually cut and polished by

207. *Isabella Rossellini photographed for* Amica *in 1991 wearing a magnificent* Bulgari Collection Internationale *necklace created in 1990. This is formed by 84.37 carats of ruby and 674.31 carats of emerald beads embellished with diamond-set roundelles.*

208. *An emerald, sapphire, ruby and diamond necklace, from the* Bulgari Collection Internationale *(1995). The value of such a jewel relies on the combination of fine gemstones, superb workmanship and brilliant design. To achieve such a result, a work of art, some 1000 hours*

COLOUR AND FABULOUS GEMSTONES

of skilled labour were required, without taking into account the lengthy process of acquiring the right gemstones and reaching a satisfactory design. Dozens of projects were drawn up and then discarded before Paolo Bulgari settled on this version. Note the beautiful gold griglia on the reverse.

209. *Enlargement of the reverse of the central part of the gem-set necklace illustrated on the previous pages. The total weight of the seven cabochon emeralds, 38.74 carats, is engraved on the gold* griglia.

skilled lapidaries in Idar Oberstein, Germany (one of the world's centres for cutting gemstones) according to requirements; then, just before setting, the gemstones are retouched once again by lapidaries in Rome in order to guarantee a perfect fit to the mount.

The reason why Bulgari has favoured this cut is because stones fashioned in this way provide suitable accents of colours. At times, the calibrated stones are faceted as seen in the *Carré* (square) line of jewels of 1987 (ill. 205); at times, they are polished with buff tops in similar manner to the 1920s style of fashioning. In the latter case, the cut of

COLOUR AND FABULOUS GEMSTONES

211. *The design for the gem-set necklace illustrated on the previous pages is constantly referred to during the process of manufacture.*

the stone can provide contrast of colour as well as surface effect. This is used by Bulgari to great effect, especially when set as a surrounding for a large faceted gem (ill. 203). The size of the most prominent stones is further emphasised by setting close by smaller *pippoli* – tiny, round cabochon stones of contrasting colours.

A real tour de force of calibrated coloured gemstones was achieved in the *Naturalia* jewels, launched in 1991 (ill. 123, 206). This collection of jewellery is of stylised naturalistic inspiration and was conceived as a celebration of nature. Here stylised fish, birds, shells and flowers are encrusted with buff-top calibré-cut stones of the most diverse shapes, ranging from onyx to coral, from tourmaline to peridot and from amethyst to chalcedony. The resulting objects are quintessentially Bulgari in all their features: bold colour combinations, mixing of materials regardless of their intrinsic worth and employing of the calibré-cut stones.

210. *The sequence of small photographs illustrates some of the stages during the lengthy production of this fine gem-set necklace. These include: comparing the central element with the design; piercing the mount for the pavé setting; sizing the back plate; comparing various elements with the design; connecting the central elements.*

191

FROM THE IDEA TO THE FINISHED OBJECT

Ultimate perfection in a piece of jewellery is the result of a combination of design, careful choice of precious materials and impeccable workmanship. Bulgari believes this and strives to achieve it at all levels, whether on a million dollar necklace or a thousand dollar ring.

The creative process can be lengthy and often months are needed to reach a single satisfactory design. An idea is conceived and then elaborated by a team of designers working under Paolo Bulgari's guidance. Several variations are proposed, discussed and analysed in detail. Proportions, volume and balance between colours are taken into consideration, and the final choice is then made. Only one design is selected; all the remaining sketches are discarded. In the case of the cabochon sapphire and emerald necklace of 1995 (ill. 208), once the basic design had been drawn up around the fourteen cabochon gems, its variations were examined (ill. 213). One was discarded because its contour with pear-shaped drops was too fussy. Another was rejected because the rubies and the diamonds around the emeralds were not balanced. The chosen design embodies Bulgari's ideals: clean contours, rounded shapes and bold juxtaposition of colours. A similar selection was undertaken to reach the final design for a pair of matching earclips (ill. 214). Copies of the chosen design are then supplied to the workshop. Here they serve as guidelines throughout the entire process of manufacture (ill. 209-211). Often a plaster or wax model is created to study further the proportions in the three dimensions (ill. 216). Every single step of the manufacturing process, from beginning to end, is closely monitored by Bulgari. Even the minutiae are considered: "This [the jewel] we inspect many times. It must be polished just right, every hinge must work just right. It

212. *Advertisement*, Feminine Dream *campaign, 1989-91.*

213. The final design for the emerald and sapphire necklace illustrated on pages 188-191 and one of the several discarded variations.

should be the exact degree of tightness...," said Nicola Bulgari. The materials used by Bulgari are the result of a careful selection. Gemstones are chosen for their inherent beauty, often regardless of their value and they are always perfectly matched. It is not easy to find a range of gemstones that are homogeneous in colour, clarity, shape and size. Metals – gold, silver, platinum, steel – are the subject of technical research. The aim of this study is to improve the performance of the alloys during the process of manufacture. Bulgari workshops have developed an alloy of gold and base metal particularly suitable for working their jewels. This alloy helps minimise porosity in cast elements such as those forming modular jewels (ill. 218). Its increased malleability is particularly suited for the working of *Tubogas* bands, which are formed of interlocking metal strips without a solder (ill. 219). In addition, this alloy is also particularly resistant to surface abrasion. Similarly, the steel used at Bulgari is also the result of advanced technological research. Workmanship at Bulgari means exceptionally crafted and finished mounts, perfect settings for the gemstones, articulations and hinges which allow great flexibility. The result is "something soft, something you want to touch," said Omar Torres. "It must fit the body harmoniously. It must be perfectly made" (*Attenzione*, New York, February 1982).

FROM THE IDEA TO THE FINISHED OBJECT

214. *Five designs for a pair of earrings to match the necklace illustrated on pages 188-191. The final choice of the elongated version is reproduced here with its relevant side view. They illustrate the complexity and length of the creative process of designing a jewel and show that many designs have to be drawn up before the final choice can be made.*

At some times it is the gem which dictates the shape of the mount, and at other times it is the design of the mount which dictates the shape of the gem. In the latter instance, the gemstone is specifically cut to fit the setting (ill. 220). Discard of precious materials while creating a jewel is of little or no concern at Bulgari, provided the end result is perfection. This is illustrated by the case of the *Bulgari Collection Internationale* necklace (ill. 208); the seven emeralds and seven sapphires are mounted in a setting of 217 rubies, 98 baguettes and 266 brilliant-cut diamonds. The rubies and the baguette diamonds had to be re-cut to fit this particular mount, a process which involved the loss of approximately 40% of the initial weight of the stones. The original 48.76 carats of faceted rubies resulted in 28.35 carats of cabochon calibré-cut stones, while the original 14.87 carats of baguette diamonds resulted in a total of 9.81 carats of tapered stones.

Nine highly skilled craftsmen laboured on this necklace for over a thousand hours, forging the elements of the mount from gold sheets, piercing it to accommodate hundreds of gems, mounting the stones, soldering the pierced back plate, joining the elements and polishing the mount (ill. 209-211).

Unusually shaped and cut gemstones have been a long-standing

215. *The final design is sent to the workshop where expert craftsmen start to manufacture the mount from gold sheet.*

195

tradition at Bulgari, regardless of costs. In the 1960s, for example, Bulgari occasionally mounted semiprecious gemstones, such as coral and turquoise, inset with cabochon gemstones of similar outline but contrasting colour. Later, even settings and pearls were tipped with minute cabochon gemstones, the size of a pin head, known within the firm as *pippoli* (ill. 124). This is an indication of how much time and attention Bulgari is prepared to invest in every detail, even to perfect such small and apparently insignificant decorative elements.

The *Naturalia* jewels are another example of this concern: their elaborate design is encrusted with specifically cut gemstones, which are true *tours de force* for lapidaries. For example, the bracelet illustrated on page 185 is set with multicoloured gems, each distinctly shaped and individually cut to fit the scale-like pattern of the mount. Not only the creation of unique gem-set jewels requires time and

216. *The creative process can be lengthy at Bulgari, and often months are needed to reach a satisfactory design. A whole team of designers works under the guidance of Paolo Bulgari in the continuous quest for originality and wearability. Once the design of a jewel is finalised, it is not unusual for Bulgari to create wax or plaster models to further study its proportion in three dimensions.*

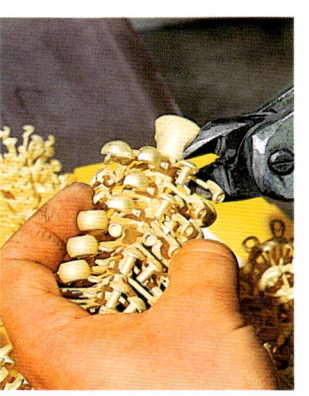

218. The different elements forming modular jewels are obtained by the process of microfusion. At Bulgari, technical research has led to the development of a gold alloy particularly suitable for this process. Its reduced porosity guarantees high standards. These images show different moments of microfusion casting.

217. At times it is the shape of an especially beautiful stone which inspires the design of a jewel. At times it is the design of a jewel which dictates the shape and cut of the stones. At Bulgari however, great care is always taken to achieve perfection in the setting. All gemstones, from precious Burmese rubies to decorative tourmalines, fit beautifully into their mounts.

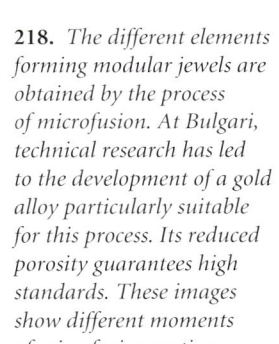

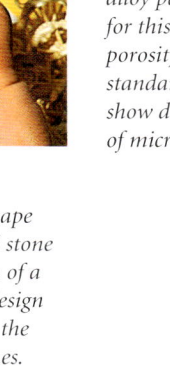

220. A hematite, gold and diamond necklace. Note the unusual cut of the diamonds, each in the shape of a letter of the alphabet. In this instance the design of the back plate is the mirror image of that of the front.

219. The high malleability of the gold alloy developed at Bulgari is ideal for the manufacture of Tubogas. Two firing processes are required to complete each jewel: one to settle the two strips of metal around the core, the second to shape the piece. These images illustrate three stages in the production of Tubogas jewels.

221. Moments in the assembling process of modular jewels. Doppio Gancio elements and pearls are joined together to form a necklace, and differently coloured gold segments, once polished, are alternated to form a Celtica bracelet.

222. *The signature "BULGARI" with a "U" continued to be used alongside the version with a "V" for decades. As late as the 1950s one finds jewels signed in this way. The pearl and diamond clip here illustrated and clearly dated 1951 confirms this practice. Setting diamond clips respectively with a white and a black or grey pearl is a typical Bulgari feature of the time.*

223. *The first signature used by the firm was "BULGARI", as illustrated by the inscription on the clasp of this diamond bracelet of the late 1920s.*

skilled labour: fine gold jewels formed by cast elements also need time and skill to be produced. Modular jewels are composed by a varying number of cast elements joined together – a *Parentesi* necklace, for example, is made of 130 elements cast from six masters. Only perfectly cast elements are used, and often as much as 50% of the production is rejected in order to comply with Bulgari's high standards. To ensure an even finish, each individual element is painstakingly polished before being assembled. The jewel, once complete with all its parts, is then given a final polish to impart the perfect finish.

Completed entirely manually, the manufacture of *Tubogas* jewels is even more laborious. Years of practice are required to train highly skilled craftsmen in this particular technique. Their ability to wrap the metal strips with an even tension around the core is essential to guarantee flexibility and durability to the jewel itself. Two firing

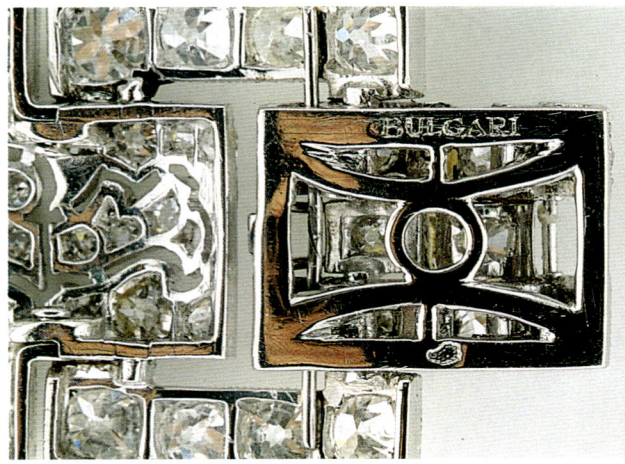
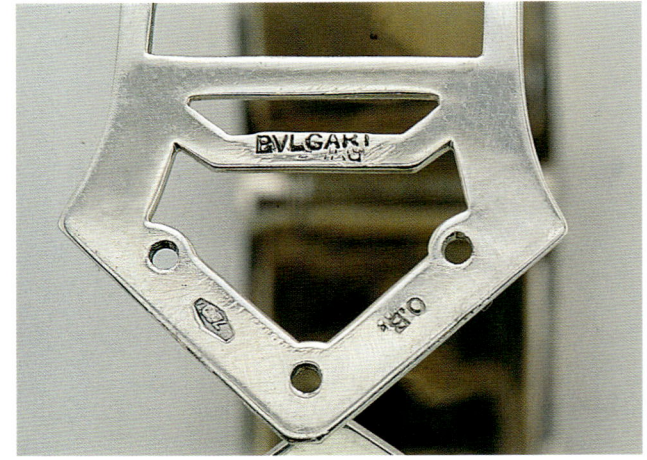
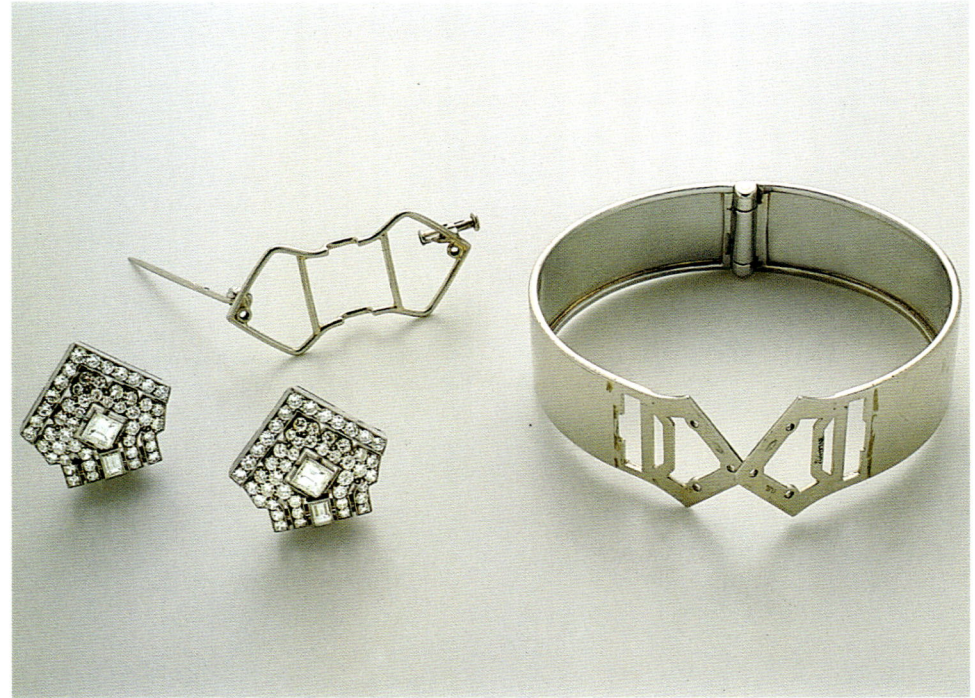

224. *It was in the 1930s that the signature "BVLGARI" with a "V" rather than a "U" was first used. The two different versions of the signature coexisted and it would appear that there was no reason for the preference of either. The signature "BVLGARI" is here stamped on the reverse of a pair of diamond lapel clips of the late 1930s, which can also be worn as the centrepiece of a bangle or as a brooch.*

227. The signature "BVLGARI" on the clasp of a Parentesi necklace set with diamond and coloured gemstones.

225. Front and back view of a pair of emerald and diamond earclips of 1995, set with 22 step-cut emeralds weighing a total of 20.31 carats and with 166 brilliant-cut diamonds for a total of 6.20 carats. The beauty and rarity of these earclips lies in the perfect match of the Colombian emeralds which are homogeneous in colour, clarity, shape and size. It can take months and sometimes years to collect the large number of matching stones necessary for the realisation of such unique jewels.

processes are required to complete a *Tubogas* jewel: the first to settle the two strips of metal around the core, the second to shape the piece. Surprisingly long strips of metal are required to create *Tubogas* jewels. In general the metal strip must be twelve to thirteen times the length of the final object: five metres of gold strip are required to make a necklace of approximately forty centimetres in length (ill. 219).

A jewel is not complete at Bulgari if its reverse has not been carefully finished as well. This is often achieved by applying a pierced metal back plate which echoes the design of the front. A gap, known as *filetto* at Bulgari, is left between the main structure of the jewel and this back plate. In some cases these plates are so elaborate, decorative and detailed that it would appear that the jewel could also be worn the other way round. This is a distinctive feature of all *Bulgari Collection Internationale* and *Naturalia* jewels.

What has been said above may be summarised by a statement made by Bulgari designer Omar Torres: "The Bulgari brothers will go ahead and spend the extra thousands of dollars it takes to do something in the most perfect way. They insist on taking the trouble. A piece that

226. The signature "BVLGARI" stamped on a pair of Alveare earclips. Note also the Italian mark "750" for the gold standard, the maker's registration number and the date of copyright for this design.

could take fifty hours to make may end up taking one hundred and fifty or two hundred hours" (*Attenzione*, New York, February 1982). Elsa Peretti, jewellery designer for Tiffany New York, had a similar view: "Bulgari creates for an audience that can afford not only the best materials, but the most painstaking and time-consuming work. Bulgari has beautiful craftsmanship. It's expensive but when you buy something with the Bulgari name, you know it is worth it"(*Attenzione*, New York, February 1982).

Marks and Signatures

All Bulgari jewels in recent times have been and continue to be signed with either a stamped or engraved "BVLGARI" logo. If from the 1970's on this has been the norm for all creations, this was not the case earlier. From surviving records it appears that the firm's first signature

228. *A pair of sapphire and diamond earclips. The signature "BVLGARI" is engraved on the mount together with the carat weight of the sapphires and the gold title "750". The hinge is also stamped "18k", an indication that these earclips had been made for the United States market. The side view shows the typical Bulgari filetto – the gap left between the jewel and the back plate.*

229. *A pair of diamond earclips. The signature "BVLGARI" is engraved on the mount together with the carat weight of the stones (respectively 2.21 and 2.07 carats) and the stock number. The earclips are also inscribed "Plat." for platinum.*

FROM THE IDEA TO THE FINISHED OBJECT

231. *The monogram "SB" used by Sotirio Bulgari to mark his silver has been retained by the firm in the form of a seal. This is applied on red wax to seal each Bulgari package, whether it is a precious jewel, a silver ornament or a perfume.*

230. *Jewels retailed outside Italy are at times stamped with additional marks for Bulgari. Those for Montecarlo ("Ste BBA"), France ("Ste BF"), Spain (monogram "BE") and Switzerland (a "BB" monogram within a hexagon) are reproduced here.*

was "BULGARI" (with a "U") (ill. 223). It was in the 1930s that the signature "BVLGARI" (with a "V") came to be used alongside the former. It would appear that there was no reason for the choice of either one of these two signatures. As late as the 1950s one still finds some jewels signed "BULGARI" (with a "U") (ill. 222, 224).

On all Bulgari creations the signature is accompanied by the title of the precious metal, stamped or engraved according to the regulations of the country of destination. For example, "750" appears on jewels destined for the Italian market, while "18k" on those for the American market. Those bound for other foreign countries are at times stamped with additional marks. Jewels and objects retailed in Switzerland bear a "BB" monogram within a hexagon; those for the Spanish market a "BE" monogram (Bulgari España). Items sold in France and Montecarlo are respectively stamped with "Ste BF" with the quatrefoil in-between and "Ste BBA" (ill. 230).

The monogram "SB" used by Sotirio Bulgari to mark his silver has been retained by the firm in the form of a seal (ill. 231). This is applied on red wax to seal each Bulgari package, whether a precious jewel, a silver ornament or a bottle of perfume. The same great care that is devoted at Bulgari to all aspects of the making of a jewel is also applied to the final presentation.

Silver and Precious Objects

The art of silversmithing is deeply rooted in the Bulgari family. As early as the beginning of the 19th century their Epirote ancestors were known as skilled silversmiths. In line with his family tradition, Sotirio Bulgari learned this craft from his father. Having left his homeland at an early age, it was thanks to his ability to work silver that he managed to develop in the 1880s a profitable business in Rome. He was known to work tirelessly from dawn until late night fusing, casting and then chasing his silver in a workshop which doubled as his home. His activity was intense to the point of compromising his health. On several occasions he continued working despite a serious medical condition. He manufactured a variety of objects and ornaments ranging from belts to buckles, from chains to chatelaines and from vinaigrettes to flatware (ill 58, 60, 61). The decorations were intricately chased and embossed in patterns which reflected Sotirio's cultural origins. These were often characterised either by figures deriving from Greek mythology or intricate scrollworks reminiscent of Byzantine gold openwork. In spite of the fact that these artefacts were not innovative in design and were of average quality, they proved to be very popular. Due to increasing demand, Sotirio soon was obliged to find assistants to help him with his work load. By the end of the 19th century he had summoned to Rome a number of Epirote silversmiths, amongst them Giannopoulos and Nessis. Examples of their work, such as the chatelaine illustrated on page 49, still exist in the Bulgari family collection.

The standard of silver employed at this time conformed to the legal Italian standard of "800", which means that the alloy consists of 800‰ pure silver and 200‰ base metal. The "800" mark to guarantee the silver standard was stamped on Sotirio's artefacts together with his

232. *Advertisement,* Dream *campaign, 1980-89.*

maker's mark which consisted of either his monogram or his initials (ill. 59). These were interchangeable and at times they were both struck on the same object.

From the turn of the century, Sotirio, besides manufacturing silver, began collecting antique European silverware, ranging from late Renaissance French to 17th-century German and 18th-century English. With Sotirio's death, the emphasis of the business shifted towards jewellery and the tradition of manufacturing silverware in house came to an end. The firm, however, continued with Costantino to expand in the area of collecting antique silver and objects, extending its range to include antique Roman silverware, a field for which Bulgari have since become world famous (ill. 18, 19, 21, 22).

The years which followed the end of the Second World War marked the firm's expansion in the area of silver to include, besides dealing in antiques, the production of high quality replicas of period pieces, such as sugar casters, candle sticks, tea pots, coffee pots and presentation dishes.

It was from the 1960s on that Bulgari began to forge, also in the field of silver, a more personal style. Bulgari's successful entry in the world of contemporary silver manufacturing is to be credited largely to Nicola Bulgari, who joined the firm in the early 1960s. In those days

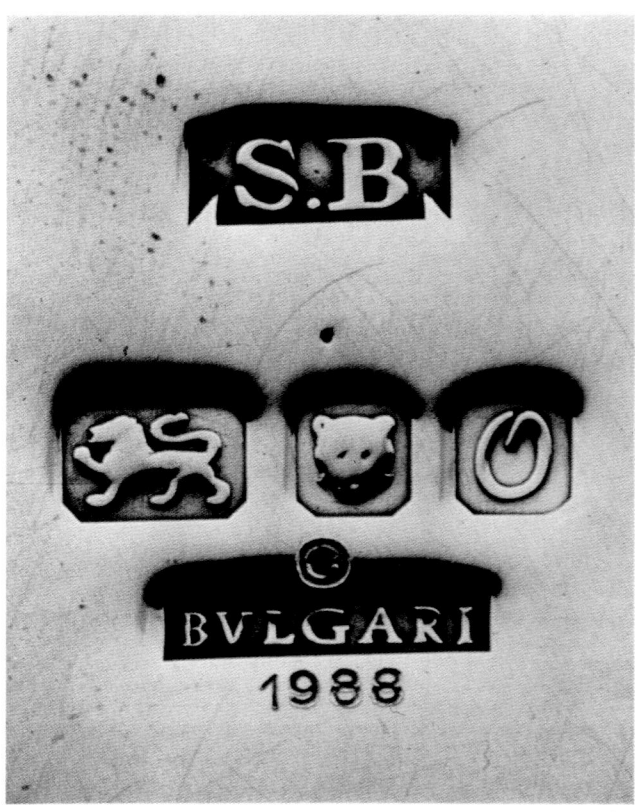

233. *Sotirio Bulgari's initials within a cartouche were registered as Bulgari's mark for silver at the Goldsmiths Hall, London, in 1967. On all Bulgari silver produced in England it appears combined with three other marks: the Lion Passant (a striding lion), the symbol for sterling silver ("925"); the leopard mask, the symbol for the London Assay Office; and the date letter (letter O indicates 1988).*

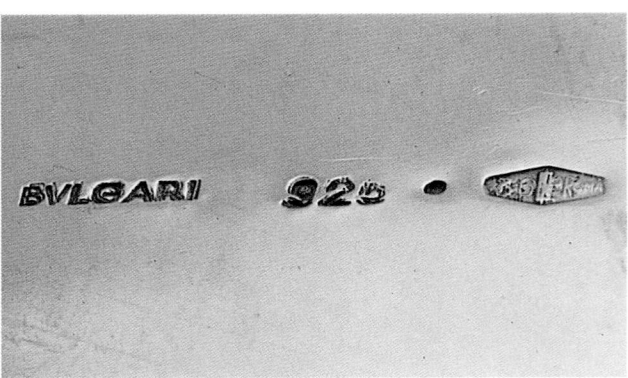

234. *Bulgari silver manufactured in Italy bears the firm's logo as its signature, the title "925" for the silver, and the maker's registration number.*

235. *A gold evening bag, decorated with a fluted pattern and embellished with a cabochon ruby thumbpiece, suspended from a red silk cord. The peculiarity of this model is the fact that it is hinged to open into two halves.*

236. *A silver tennis ball can complete with balls inscribed with the "BVLGARI" logo is just one among the many whimsical silver creations introduced by the firm from the late 1960s on.*

his uncle Costantino, an eminent scholar in the field of antique silver, and author of *Argentieri, Gemmari e Orafi d'Italia*, a major work on Italian gold and silversmiths, used to take Nicola on buying expeditions. This experience developed Nicola's understanding for antique silver and, at the same time, led him to mature a conviction that Bulgari should not only be the receptacle of rare antique objects, but also the creator of fine modern silverware. Nicola realised that Bulgari's mission was the creation of modern silverware of high artistic value. He viewed the production of modern silver as a continuation of the great traditions of the past and also a legacy for the future, provided that it was based on fine design and outstanding quality. In a later interview (*Argento!*, March 1991) Nicola Bulgari confirmed his views: "*Bisogna inserirsi nel filone della storia, comprendere il passato ed usarlo come base per proiettarsi nel futuro*" ("One has to penetrate the course of history, understand the past, and use this knowledge as a foundation for the future").

Bulgari's quest to reach perfection led the firm to abandon the traditional Italian silver standard of 800 in favour of a finer title. They opted for sterling silver, a finer alloy consisting of 925‰ pure silver and 75‰ base metal. The use of sterling silver – obligatory in Britain but unusual for an Italian firm – allowed Bulgari in 1967 to register its

237. *A group of silver Colonna objects including: a coffee pot, a vase and a table clock, whose design is inspired by the bold simplicity of ancient Doric columns – hence the name of the line. The adaptations of an antique architectural element to the design of a 20th-century object of everyday use is yet another example of Bulgari's reverence for the past and of its ability to reinterpret it into something actual and contemporary.*

mark at the London Goldsmiths Hall. This is the headquarters of the prestigious guild of Goldsmiths, an institution which has been active in Britain since 1327 and controls the standard of precious metals. The fact that Bulgari was admitted as a member of such an exclusive and illustrious institution – one of the few non-English members and indeed the only Italian – is a clear sign of international recognition of Bulgari's work in the field of silver. The registered mark consists of the initials "SB", in use since the time of Sotirio. To comply with the strict regulations of the Guild, this is accompanied by three other marks: the *Lion Passant* (a striding lion), the symbol for sterling silver; the leopard mask, the symbol for the London Assay Office; and a date letter (ill. 233). The complexity of the mark is intended to guarantee the authenticity and quality of the piece.

During this decade, Bulgari introduced a range of modern and unusual silver objects, such as vases modelled after terracotta flowerpots, tumblers shaped and engraved as the traditional Coca Cola glass, and wine carafes shaped as those used in Italian trattorias. Silver paperweights designed as postage stamps, silver postcards and telegrams ready to be engraved with personal messages and tennis ball cans stamped "BVLGARI" were whimsical and successful additions to its modern silver range (ill. 236).

238. *A group of* Olimpia *silver objects including: a coffee pot, a tea pot, a milk jug and a sugar bowl. Bulgari's modern silver characteristically relies on simple yet recognisable shapes where the decoration is an integral part of the design.*

From the late 1970s, in line with its development of modular jewellery, Bulgari started to produce ranges of silver objects, whose common denominator were simple yet recognisable shapes in which the decoration is an integral part of the design. Just as modular jewellery relied on decorative motifs which could be adapted and repeated to form a multiplicity of ornaments, in the same manner Bulgari's modern silver was characterised by a design that could be adapted to a variety of objects: from ashtrays to vases, from place-card holders to book-ends, from picture frames to coffee pots, from hourglasses to moneyclips, from paperknives to salt cellars, from trays to book markers, from boxes to keyrings.

The first line to be created, in 1979, was the *Colonna* (column), inspired by the bold simplicity of ancient Doric columns (ill. 237). As all Bulgari creations of this time, *Colonna* silver is also characterised by sleek contours, rounded edges, volume and substantial weight. The adaptation of an antique architectural element to the design of a 20th-century object of everyday use is yet another example of Bulgari's reverence for the past and of its ability to reinterpret it into something actual and contemporary.

Since the creation of the *Colonna* silver, Bulgari has applied similar criteria to other lines, such as *Olimpia*, of 1988, reminiscent of the

SILVER AND PRECIOUS OBJECTS

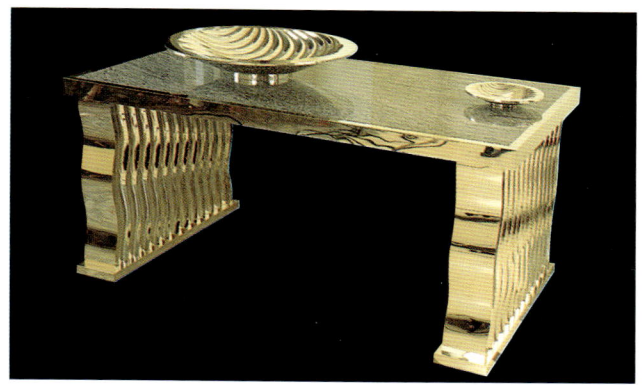

240. *A silver* Onda *table (weighing 18 kilograms) and two bowls of the same line, designed in 1994, illustrate how at Bulgari the same decorative motif, which is integral part of the design, can be adapted and repeated to form a multiplicity of objects.*

design of an Olympic stadium, *Onda* (wave) of 1990, and *Cerniera* (hinge) of 1992 (ill 238, 240, 241).

Quality of manufacture together with fine design are of paramount importance at Bulgari. The silver sheets employed in the construction of an object are always surprisingly thick. Their weight conveys the typical Bulgari feature of solidity and substance. The soldering is impeccable, rendered even more arduous by the use of such thick sheets of silver. The finish is superb, even the reverse of an object is beautifully crafted and polished to the highest standards. The same attention is given to all parts of an object, even if they are concealed, including bases and interiors.

The ultimate product is, for Bulgari, of primary importance regardless of what it takes in terms of time, cost and effort. For example the creative process which led to the realisation of the prototype *Borromini* table centrepiece (1987) spanned over two years. During this time numerous difficulties were encountered, and on

239. *A whimsical silver tray modelled after those used in Italian patisseries to package cakes.*

241. *A silver* Onda *(wave) centrepiece. This line of silverware, created in 1990, is characterised by a sinuous decorative pattern, hence the name.*

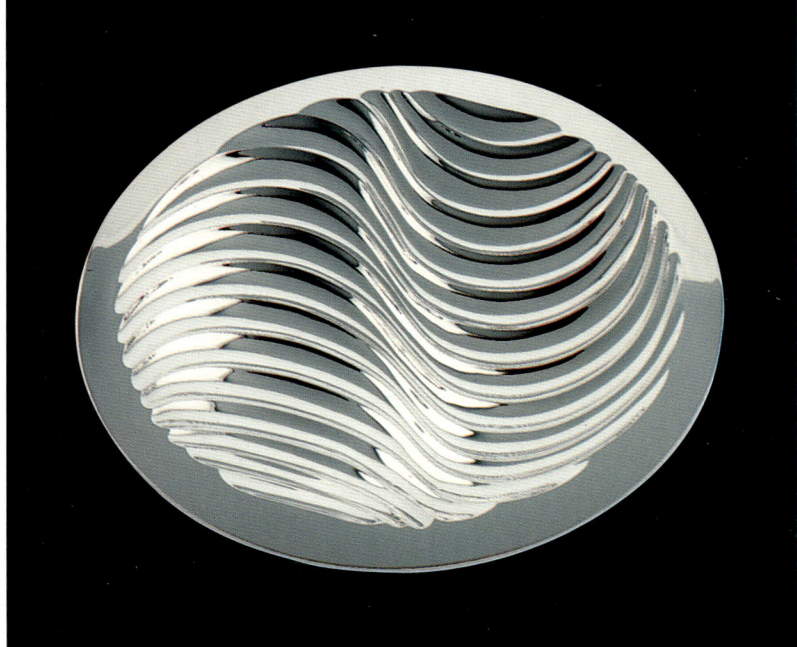

209

242. *A silver* Borromini *table centrepiece, 1987. The scalloped bowl characterised by layered and jagged contours was a technical feat by the hands of Roman silvermasters. It is a fine example of how silver comes to life at Bulgari thanks to the constant play of light, reflected from the smooth concave and convex surfaces.*

various occasions Bulgari was tempted to drop the project entirely. This lengthy process resulted in a silver scalloped bowl, characterised by layered and jagged contours (ill. 242) – a modern and streamlined interpretation of the articulated and convoluted shapes favoured by Baroque architect Borromini. In this particular example Bulgari managed to achieve perfect proportions and overcome the technical difficulties posed by the soldering of such thick silver sheets into perfectly clean edges. The *Borromini* falls within a series of table centrepieces which derive inspiration from the past. The *Boscoreale* bowl, based on Roman silverware of the 1st century AD, now in the Archaeological Museum in Naples, was created in 1967.

This was followed, in 1989, by the *Siracusa* bowl, inspired by an ancient ceramic dish found in Sicily and held in Syracuse Archaeological Museum. Together with the *Borromini*, these bowls form the core of a collection known as the *Collezione Archeologica* (Archaeological Collection).

The technical perfection of all Bulgari silver is the result of a successful marriage between the skills of silversmiths trained in the finest Italian and British traditions. The outstanding achievements of Bulgari in the field of silver creations have been largely possible thanks to the close and long-standing association with silver masters

SILVER AND PRECIOUS OBJECTS

Vitali of Rome, a collaboration which spanned four generation. Vitali's input has been a determining factor in both the technical and artistic aspects of Bulgari silver. All items manufactured for Bulgari in Italy bear the "925" mark for the silver title, Bulgari's logo as signature, and the maker's registration number. Those produced in England bear the "BVLGARI" logo and are struck with the official London Assay marks (ill. 233, 234).

A feat of technical and artistic virtuosity resulted in 1994 in the creation of the first modern Bulgari flatware set (ill. 243). It is comprised of 77 basic pieces characterised by a perfectly proportioned streamlined sinuous design. The weight of these forks, spoons and knives is substantial and well distributed. They are easy to use as well as pleasing to the eye. This is yet another example of Bulgari's constant concern that an ornament – whether a jewel or an object – has to be beautiful but also functional. A piece of jewellery has to be comfortable to wear and a silver object has to be practical to use; neither should be relegated to a safe. Speaking about silver, Nicola Bulgari said, "Silver should not be left to die in a cabinet..., silver is not only for display but above all to be used" (*Argento!*, March 1991).

The mission which Nicola Bulgari set out to fulfil from the 1960s onwards in the field of silver is in the process of being achieved. Undoubtedly modern Bulgari silver creations are invaluable and

243. *A silver canteen of 1994 comprising seventy-seven pieces: these are characterised by a perfectly proportioned sinuous design and a carefully studied weight, which make them not only beautiful to look at but also easy to handle. At Bulgari they believe that "silver is not only for display but above all to be used" (Argento!, March 1991).*

timeless contributions to the long-standing tradition of fine silver. Already one of its creations – the *Borromini* table centrepiece – is housed since 1988 in the prestigious permanent collection of the Goldsmiths Hall in London, an undisputed sign of the highest international recognition.

Luxury Accessories

Over the decades, Bulgari has created a number of fine ornaments which bridge the gap between an everyday object and a fine jewel. The *Bugnato* jewelled table clocks of 1990 are a successful rendering of this merging of the functional with the superfluous (ill. 244). These eight timepieces were conceived as miniature façades based on a reinterpretation of architectural features of Italian Renaissance *palazzi*. Each is encrusted with gemstones: amethyst, red coral, mother-of-pearl, brown and yellow citrines, fashioned to simulate *Bugnato* (rustication) masonry typical of Renaissance architecture. These creations are yet another manifestation of Bulgari's ability to reinterpret elements of the past in a modern key. Just as Bulgari revives classical antiquity in its jewels by setting them with ancient coins or adapts the motif of ancient Greek Doric columns to its silverware, in these timepieces the firm, equally successfully, re-elaborates elements from Italian Renaissance.

SILVER AND PRECIOUS OBJECTS

This clearly reflects Bulgari's awareness and understanding of the past and its cultural origins which stem from the Mediterranean world. In addition, Bulgari's attitude towards the past reflects a contemporary and global phenomenon: Post-modernism.

Gianni Bulgari was aware of this when he said, "movements such as Post-modernism are a clear indication of a trend towards the recovery of the past and of a taste for ornamentation of which we have been deprived due to an ideological misunderstanding" (*Arbiter*, March-April 1982).

Another successful marriage between a utilitarian object and a jewel was achieved by Bulgari with the creation of its unmistakable evening bag, designed in the early 1960s in the form of an oval gold case. Its success relied on its simple form characterised by a rounded outline and a strong sense of volume which differed from the more conventional jewelled evening bags of the time. It came in a variety of finishes and decorations, including tortoiseshell, enamel, gemstones and coins. Certainly the most popular was and still is the fluted gold model. All are suspended on silk cords completed by tassels, which are supplied in a variety of colours and can be changed to match different outfits. Their popularity was such that at times it was not uncommon for Bulgari to have a waiting list for such bags – the ultimate luxury accessory (ill. 158, 235).

244. *Six from a group of eight gold and gem-set table clocks (1990) from the* Bugnato *line. Conceived as miniature façades based on a reinterpretation of architectural features of Italian Renaissance palazzi, these timepieces bridge the gap between everyday objects and fine jewels.*

Watches

Although it is likely that Bulgari retailed watches from the very beginning of its business, the first existing examples and watch designs date back to the 1920s.

As did most jewellers of the time, Bulgari designed and manufactured wristwatches and lapel watches and fitted them with movements made by the prominent timepiece makers of the day. The emphasis was on the design and on the precious setting rather than on the movement itself. The design of these early jewelled watches was in keeping with the current trends of Art Déco style as illustrated by the onyx, black enamel and diamond lapel watch on page 57 and by the designs for gem-set wristwatches on page 56.

Gentlemen's watches also followed this pattern as is confirmed by the elegant gold pocket watch signed by Bulgari and fitted with a movement by Audemars Piguet et Cie. This was purchased in 1938 by Count Galeazzo Ciano di Cortellazzo, husband of Mussolini's daughter Edda and, at the time, Minister for Foreign Affairs in Italy. Known for his style and elegance, Ciano was one of Bulgari's regular clients until his death in 1944. This particular purchase, acquired for the sum of 8,000 liras, is recorded in the firm's ledger as entry n. 69 dated 9 July 1938: "*1 orologio uomo in oro*" (ill. 246, 247).

The beginning of Bulgari's success in the field of watches dates back to the late 1940s and coincided with the firm's retailing of wristwatches in the form of snakes. These were designed as gold coiled serpents worn wrapped around the wrist, which terminated with a jewelled head concealing the dial. These sinuous and flexible snake bracelet-watches are a 20th-century interpretation of a long-standing tradition. The serpent, symbol of wisdom, life, and eternity, has wound its way through the history of jewellery design since antiquity. In Hellenistic

245. *Advertisement,* Metamorphosis *campaign, 1992-96.*

246. *A gold pocket-watch by Bulgari, 1930s, mounted with an Audemars Piguet movement. As most jewellers of the time, Bulgari manufactured lapel, pocket and wristwatches and fitted them with movements made by prominent timepiece makers of the day. This watch was purchased by Galeazzo Ciano as a gift to celebrate the nomination of his colleague Ottavio De Peppo as Italian ambassador to Turkey. De Peppo had served in the Ministry for Foreign Affairs under Ciano for four years. The dates relating to his service from the twelfth to the sixteenth year of the Fascist era are inscribed on the reverse as well as the simulated signature of Ciano.*

and Roman times, gold serpent bracelets were frequently worn as ornaments and as talismans. This fashion went into decline and was resumed in the mid-19th century when the snake motif, worn around the neck or the arm, was rendered as a flexible chain often paved with gemstones such as turquoises. In the 1890s, serpents once more came to the forefront of jewellery design in the guise of sinister enamelled creatures by the hands of Art Nouveau jewellers.

The original three coil gold snake wristwatch decorated with diamonds soon became a Bulgari best seller (ill. 248). In the 1950s and 1960s a number of variations were added. These included polychrome enamel examples of variously designed scale-like linking of three or more coils, at times decorated with gemstones.

In the 1970s the snake wristwatch evolved into a much more stylised form, consisting of plain flexible spirals devoid of head and tail. The

247. *A page from Bulgari's purchase record book of 1938 reporting Count Galeazzo Ciano as the buyer of the gold pocket-watch illustrated above.*

unconcealed dial became a feature of these new wristwatches. All shapes of dials were employed, from round to octagonal, from oval to rectangular; the finest movements were selected, such as Audemars Piguet, Jaeger-Le Coultre, Vacheron Constantin and Movado. These new stylised snake wristwatches were rendered in gold *Tubogas* linking and gold and blackened steel mesh-work. This simplification of the snake form is perhaps one of the most poignant manifestations of the stylisation of naturalistic motifs, which became a central theme of Bulgari's work in the early 1970s (ill. 249-251).

Although Bulgari had been selling watches since the 1920s, it was only in the late 1970s that the firm launched its own first important watch collection. The success was such that it prompted, in 1982, the firm to found "Bulgari Time" in Switzerland, a company with the sole responsibility of overseeing the creation and production of all Bulgari

248. *A gold and diamond bracelet-watch by Bulgari designed as a serpent. This model, created in the late 1940s, marked the beginning of the success of Bulgari in the field of wristwatches. The supple and flexible body is of polished yellow gold, the tail and head are set with diamonds. The movement, by Movado, is concealed in the jewelled head.*

249. *A gold, black enamel, diamond and ruby snake bracelet-watch, and a gold and blackened steel wristwatch formed by a coiled band of basket weave design with an Audemars Piguet movement, 1970s.*

watches. Since 1989 the technical research relating to the production of watch movements has been a joint venture with Girard Perregaux Manufacture, one of the oldest and most respected Swiss watchmakers. This association has led to a constant improvement and sophistication of Bulgari timepieces. Each watch is made according to the most rigid qualitative criteria: Swiss movement, scratch-resistant sapphire crystal, and water-resistant crown and case.

The firm's best-known wristwatch, the BVLGARI-BVLGARI, was launched in 1977. Its case is formed by a horizontal cross section of a cylinder, 5 mm in height, and its black enamel dial is framed by a gold band inscribed twice with the "BVLGARI" logo. This highly successful design originated from an earlier digital gold watch which was inscribed along the rim "BVLGARI ROMA" (ill. 252).

This model was produced in 1975 as a limited series of 100 examples intended as gifts for Bulgari clients. The unexpected success of such a limited, promotional line of watches led Bulgari to adopt the same casing for mechanical watches and then in 1977 to create and launch the BVLGARI-BVLGARI wristwatch.

The success of this timepiece was immediate and the BVLGARI-BVLGARI, in all its declination, continues to be the firm's best-selling wristwatch (ill. 253).

250. *A group of eight bracelet-watches of the 1970s showing variations on the snake bracelet motif. These are either decorated with polychrome enamel and gemstones, or are characterised by a much more stylised form, where the dials become a feature of the design. In these latter examples the bracelet is either a coil of Tubogas or an elaborate woven band. Note the chromatic contrast achieved by the juxtaposition of differently coloured metals such as gold and blackened steel.*

252. A gold digital wristwatch of 1975, inscribed in relief on the bezel "BVLGARI ROMA", one from a limited series of 100 examples intended as gifts to Bulgari clients. The success of this digital watch was such that it became the model for the BVLGARI-BVLGARI watch of 1977.

This design is produced in four sizes to suit men and women and is available with mechanical or quartz movement and with or without date aperture. The original yellow gold version with hand-stitched tan leather strap was followed by a steel version combined with variously coloured leather and crocodile straps. In line with Bulgari's desire to create a family of clearly recognisable ornaments, the BVLGARI-BVLGARI watch also underwent a process of "declination." This resulted in the BVLGARI-BVLGARI gold watch being fitted with gold or gold and steel integral bracelets. Similarly, the steel version was fitted with an integral steel bracelet for the sporty occasions, while diamond encrusted dials were created to meet the requirements of formal events. In addition, the BVLGARI-BVLGARI has been set in a variety of *Tubogas* bracelets resulting in the ultimate Bulgari jewel of the 1980's (ill. 178). Since 1977 the "BVLGARI" logo has featured prominently in the design for other watches. At times its rendering is identical to the logo on the watch of 1977, as for example on the *Chronograph*, the *Sports Line* and the plastic and gold wristwatches, while at other times there are some variations as seen on the *Anfiteatro* and the *Quadrato* watches. The nearly ubiquitous logo is not surprisingly used as a decorative device, as one of the firm's main concerns since the late 1970s has been to create designs which are unmistakably Bulgari.

The "BVLGARI BVLGARI" logo is central to the decoration of the bezel of chronographs (1990) with quartz movement and mechanical functions and to *Sports Line* wristwatches (1994) with automatic movements, black dials and fluorescent indexes (ill. 259). These are produced in a variety of materials: gold, gold and steel, and steel with various metal and leather straps. Paolo Bulgari, commenting on the Sports watches, said: "For this new range of watches, the main thing

251. A group of nine bracelet-watches of the 1970s, in a stylised serpent design. Characteristically, the dials become a feature of the design and the coiled bracelet are of Tubogas or brick-work pattern.

is that they are practical and there are also the echoes of the BVLGARI-BVLGARI watch, so it is an evolution, not a revolution."

Furthermore, in 1993 the firm launched a limited series of black plastic and gold BVLGARI-BVLGARI watches on tan leather straps. Each Bulgari shop worldwide received a limited quantity of such watches, each numbered and inscribed with the name of the city where the shop is located. The peculiarity of this model is the daring juxtaposition of plastic and gold combined with a transparent back-case revealing the automatic movement (ill. 258). "We are delighted to introduce this new and fun version of our classic wristwatch," said Paolo Bulgari. "While respecting the original design, we have succeeded in being creative in the choice of materials and in obtaining a very high degree of quality." This watch had such an overwhelming success that it sold out in a very short period of time. It is already considered a collector's

253. *The gold* BVLGARI-BVLGARI *watch in its four sizes is one of the firm's trademarks and is fitted with quartz or mechanical movement. Its success is based on its clean shape combined with the "*BVLGARI*" logo featured as a decorative device. Recognisable and well conceived designs are cornerstones in all areas of Bulgari's production.*

item and examples have already been included in international watch and jewellery auctions, commanding high prices.

In 1989 the BVLGARI-BVLGARI wristwatch was followed by the *Anfiteatro*, characterised by a concave bezel reminiscent of the shape of ancient Greek amphitheatres, hence the name. Like its forerunner, this watch also relies on the use of the "BVLGARI" logo as a decorative device, though it is less prominent, as it is subtly engraved on the concave bezel. The success of this watch is to be found in the combination of the decorative use of the logo with the pure, simple design of classical inspiration, another example of Bulgari's successful marriage between the contemporary and the antique. The champagne coloured dial of the traditional version is combined with yellow gold, while the platinum version is characterised by a white dial and, since 1995, examples are at times also encrusted with diamonds (ill. 254). A limited series of 500 gold and 100 platinum *Anfiteatro* watches was fitted with automatic movement.

In 1992 Bulgari launched the *Quadrato* (square) wristwatch, unusual for its angularity, a feature which had not been utilised by the firm before this time. The "BVLGARI" logo continues to be engraved on the watch, though discreetly placed on the side of the case, in line with the understated trend which has characterised the firm since the early

254. *Two gold* Anfiteatro *wristwatches, one encrusted with diamonds. This model, created in 1989, is characterised by a concave bezel reminiscent of the shape of ancient Greek amphitheatres, hence the name. The success of this watch is to be found in the combination of the decorative use of the logo with the pure, simple design of classical inspiration: another example of Bulgari's successful marriage of the contemporary and the antique.*

1990s. The *Quadrato*, made of yellow gold or steel with a black dial, is available in three sizes, with or without date aperture and with quartz or mechanical movement. Leather straps and metal bracelets are combined with this model (ill. 255). Since 1995, the *Quadrato* includes a number of precious variations: the bezel and dial encrusted with diamonds on a leather strap, bezel and dial in gold and diamonds on a similarly decorated bracelet, and finally bezel, dial and bracelet respectively set with emeralds, rubies and sapphires embellished with diamonds; all with quartz movements and water-resistant cases (ill. 256).

A particularly important year in the history of Bulgari watches was 1994 as it marked the expansion of the firm in the field of sport timepieces with the *Scuba* and Bulgari's entry into the world of fine horology with the launch of *Grandes Complications* creations (ill. 262).

255. A Quadrato *steel wristwatch. Launched in 1992, this angular model features the "*BVLGARI*" logo on the side of the case. Produced either in gold or steel, it is provided with quartz or mechanical movement. Since 1995 this model also includes a number of variations entirely encrusted with precious gems.*

256. *Three* Quadrato *bracelet-watches of 1995, lavishly encrusted with diamonds, rubies, sapphires and emeralds.*

The main inspiration behind the new Bulgari *Grandes Complications* watches is the same inspiration that lies at the foundation of all Bulgari creations: the desire to combine fine quality and modern design. The *Tourbillon* and the *Répétition Minutes* (minute repeater) are addressed to those who seek timepieces with sophisticated movements: they can be regarded as true works of art for their technical features which are the result of months of skilled labour. Made to order, they are produced in limited numbers by "Bulgari Time" expert watchmakers in Neuchâtel, Switzerland.

The principle of the *Tourbillon*, patented by Abraham-Louis Breguet in 1801, offered an innovative solution to eliminate errors of rate in the vertical position. Even today this complex mechanism is made exclusively thanks to the expertise and ability of a small number of watchmakers and guarantees a highly precise performance.

This complex movement is enclosed in an *Anfiteatro* case either of gold or platinum, and the face is characterised by an aperture which reveals the movement and allows the rotation of the balance-wheel to be admired. The crown is water-resistant and the sapphire crystal is anti-scratch.

The *Répétition Minutes* movement is one of the most beautiful and sophisticated clock mechanisms. Its charm is revealed when the chime button is activated and two crystalline chimes sound to strike hours, quarters and minutes. Also enclosed in an *Anfiteatro* case, the *Répétition Minutes* is available in yellow gold and platinum. The secrets of this precious movement are at times revealed in a version of the watch with a transparent back-case in sapphire crystal.

The *Scuba*, a diver's watch, is water resistant up to 200 metres deep and has an automatic movement with a COSC chronometric

257. *"Bulgari Time" workshop, Neuchâtel (Switzerland). The two watches in the process of being completed are a* Tourbillon *and a* Sports Line.

258. *The transgressive black plastic and gold wristwatch of 1993, another variation on the BVLGARI-BVLGARI theme. A feature of this limited series of watches is the inscription of the name of the city where the retailing Bulgari shop is located. The transparent back of this model enables one to view the gold automatic movement.*

certification. This guarantees that the watch lives up to the high standards of the Official Swiss Chronometer Board. Their certification test lasts for several weeks and the certificate is only awarded after a series of rigorous tests that have been performed on each individual watch. In addition, the *Scuba* has fluorescent hands and numerals and date aperture at 3 o'clock. Made of gold and steel or steel, it is combined with integral metal bracelets or natural rubber straps and is addressed to a discerning market requiring a sport timepiece of high precision and stylish design. In 1995 the range was extended to include also a *Scuba Chrono* (ill. 260).

Watches have also featured prominently in Bulgari modular jewellery. The first watch mounted in a *Parentesi* penannular bangle dates back to 1985 (see page 137). A second jewelled bracelet-watch was created in 1989 for the *Alveare* modular line, characterised by a hexagonal dial which echoes the stylised honeycomb pattern of this module. Both *Parentesi* and *Alveare* bracelet-watches, in line with the modular concept of jewellery, are available in a variety of materials ranging from plain gold, gold and steel, and gold and diamonds.

In 1990 the *Antalia* was added to the range of Bulgari women's jewelled bracelet-watches. Though strictly speaking not part of a modular line, this model is characterised by a gold hinged penannular

259. *A steel Chronograph with integral bracelet and a* Sports Line *watch in gold. These examples illustrate how the* BVLGARI-BVLGARI *concept has also been successfully adapted since 1990 to sports watches. Paolo Bulgari, commenting on this line, stated that it was an evolution of the* BVLGARI-BVLGARI *design, not a revolution.*

260. *Created in 1994, the* Scuba *diver's watch is water-resistant up to 200 metres deep and has an automatic movement with COSC chronometric certification. This steel example is mounted on a natural rubber strap.*

261. *Three variations of gold and diamond* Trika *bracelet-watches. Created in 1995, this model is characterised by an extremely flexible bracelet, composed by 187 elements forming a braid design, hence the name* Trika *(Greek for braid).*

bangle which may be covered by variously coloured interchangeable leather straps.

1995 saw the launch of *Trika*, another fine jewelled bracelet-watch for women (ill. 261). It is characterised by an entirely new design: the case is square with rounded edges, the sapphire crystal is convex and the dial, decorated with a gold circle, is pavé-set with brilliant-cut

262. *The year 1994 marked the entry of Bulgari into the world of fine horology with the launch of two* Grandes Complications *creations: the* Tourbillon *and the* Répétition Minutes. *These timepieces are addressed to a discerning public seeking watches with highly sophisticated movements. These can be regarded as true works of art for their technical features and are enclosed in elegant gold or platinum* Anfiteatro *cases. The beauty of their sophisticated movements is not concealed but, on the contrary, is displayed to great advantage. The rotation of the balance wheel of the* Tourbillon *is visible through an aperture on the dial, while at times a transparent reverse allows the secrets of the complex movement of the* Répétition Minutes *to be seen.*

diamonds. The novelty also consists in its extremely flexible bracelet characterised by a braid motif, hence the name *Trika* – Greek for braid – a feature which departs from the former rigid bangle watches. This elegant model is always rendered with a diamond-set dial and a choice of three different bracelets: either plain gold, or gold with diamond-set lines – which underline the intricacy of the braided pattern, or entirely paved with diamonds.

The success of Bulgari watches is reflected by the fact that watch sales account, at the end of the 20th century, for nearly half the firm's turnover. As in the field of jewellery, Bulgari has not undermined its high standards of design and manufacture in the process of widening its market of timepieces. All watches are wearable, modern, and recognisable as Bulgari; they range from 2,000 to 250,000 dollars and therefore are available to a wide but discerning public.

Perfumes

Bulgari's desire to expand the awareness of its name beyond the boundaries of jewels and watches crystallised in 1990 in the creation of "Bulgari Parfums" in Neuchâtel, Switzerland, a company entirely dedicated to the creation, production and distribution of all Bulgari fragrances. 1992 saw the launch of *Eau Parfumée, Cologne au thé vert*, a fresh green tea fragrance, a forerunner of the increasingly popular fragrances suitable both for men and women. The same care and time devoted to the making of jewellery was dedicated by Bulgari also to the creation of this scent. Two years of research were spent to create the fragrance, to design its bottle and to choose its name. *Eau Parfumée*, with its top note of Italian bergamot, Spanish orange blossom, Ceylon cardamom, Jamaican pepper, Russian coriander, its middle note of Bulgarian rose and Egyptian jasmine, and its base note of green tea and smoked wood, is a pleasantly sweet and flowery fragrance. Yet it is gently citrussy and fresh, typical for its discreet, unobtrusive and non-aggressive character. *Eau Parfumée* is a perfect combination of traditional Mediterranean fragrances such as bergamot, orange blossom, rose and jasmine which are revealed as soon as this scent is worn, and more unusual, Oriental notes such as that of green tea. The latter develops slowly and gives a lasting and refreshing feeling of well-being. The simple and linear design of the bottle, a tall cylinder enhanced by the use of frosted glass, is an ideal complement to the unobtrusive character of this scent. The silver coloured stopper, with a frosted glass plaque, is decorated with the engraved "BVLGARI" logo. As for the fragrance itself, the design of the bottle is the result of a process of elimination of various projects in favour of a simple and elegant shape.

The clean lines, the volume and the use of the "BVLGARI" logo which

263. *Advertisement, 1994.*

characterise this bottle are features common to all Bulgari creations. The success of *Eau Parfumée* has encouraged "Bulgari Parfums" to continue to work on new fragrances. In 1994 BVLGARI *pour Femme*, a scent exclusively for women, was launched. This is characterised by fresh notes which develop into a flowery fragrance dominated by Sambac jasmine tea and by the sensual notes of Grasse mimosa. Bulgari's complex perfume, clearly recognisable yet discreet and non-aggressive, is characterised by top notes of Brazilian wood, Nossi-Be ylang-ylang, orange blossom and Italian bergamot, middle note of jasmine tea, mimosa and rose, and base note of iris, vetiver and musk. In touch with Bulgari's use of declining a design into multiple variations as seen in the modular jewellery, the bottle of BVLGARI *pour Femme* is a variation of that of *Eau Parfumée*: shorter, elliptical in section, with a gold stopper. Sensual but not ostentatious, flowery yet fresh, unusual for its note of jasmine tea, BVLGARI *pour Femme* was created, as Paolo Bulgari said, "as a tribute to women, as an answer to their desire to rediscover luxury and find it renewed and different, characterised by understatement and absolute quality." To contain this precious scent

264. *Bulgari launched its first scent,* Eau Parfumée, *in 1992. This unobtrusive fragrance is contained in a simple and linear bottle: a tall frosted glass cylinder with a silver coloured stopper, characteristically decorated with the "*BVLGARI*" logo.*

265. *The design of the Bulgari bottle of scents is the result of a process of elimination of different proposals. The bottle designed in 1994 to contain the scent* BVLGARI *pour Femme is a modified version of the* Eau Parfumée *bottle.*

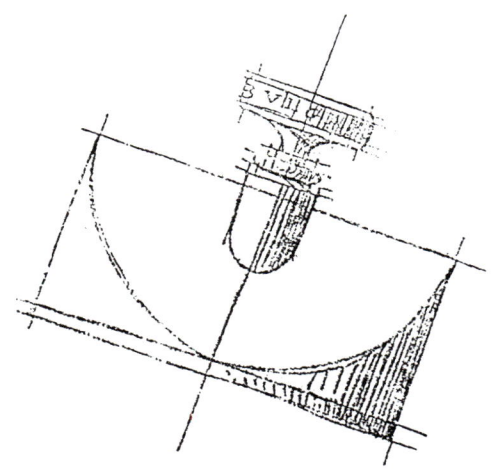

266. BVLGARI *pour Homme was launched in 1995. Characteristically, its bottle and packaging are a variation of those for other Bulgari fragrances.*

and enhance its unique notes, Bulgari created, in collaboration with master glassmaker Carlo Moretti from Murano, a special and precious collection of bottles. These colourful Venetian glass bottles in different shapes are produced in a limited and numbered series of 100 examples. They are as beautiful, as perfectly crafted and desirable as a Bulgari jewel. Characteristically, their silver stopper is engraved with the "BVLGARI" logo. These bottles are presented in an elegant blue leather box, which doubles as a jewellery box.

In 1995 the range of Bulgari fragrances expanded to include *BVLGARI pour Homme*, characterised by an innovative combination of exotic Darjeeling tea, Mediterranean bergamot and orange blossom.

The same care that has been devoted to the creation of fragrances and their bottles has been applied to their packaging. This consists of environmentally friendly cardboard boxes in pale colours: yet another manifestation of Bulgari's concern with current environmental issues and understatement typical of the 1990s. "Bulgari Parfums" is part of a much wider project that the firm has been pursuing for the last decade. The aim is to create a wider international awareness of the name Bulgari. The production and worldwide distribution of fragrances has not altered Bulgari's philosophy of high quality and exclusivity; on the contrary, it has guaranteed availability to a larger audience.

267. *Murano glass master Carlo Moretti created a special collection of crystal bottles of different shapes and colours to present the fragrance* BVLGARI *pour Femme. Each bottle has a silver stopper engraved with the "*BVLGARI*" logo and is supplied with a miniature silver funnel.*

Bvlgari's Image

Creating an Empire

From modest beginnings in Epirus, Bulgari family set up its empire with extraordinary speed and determination, much like Alexander the Great, who from those lands within a few years established a vast empire stretching over three continents – Europe, Africa and Asia. From the 1970s on, the flagship shop in Via dei Condotti in Rome began to be supported by an ever growing international network of Bulgari outlets. This was the culmination of one of Giorgio's dreams: to export Bulgari production to the entire world.

The first and most important shops in New York (1970) and Geneva (1974) are now joined by numerous others. In Europe there are shops in Montecarlo (1977), Paris (two outlets; first opened 1979), Milan (1986), London (three outlets; first opened 1988), Munich (1989), St Moritz (1989), Madrid (1991), Cortina d'Ampezzo (1992), Düsseldorf (1992), Zurich (1993), Cannes (1993), Athens (1993), Berlin (1995) and Florence (1995). In the United States of America, in New York (second outlet, 1989), in Aspen (1991), Los Angeles (1992), San Francisco (1992), Miami (1992), Las Vegas (1993), Costa Mesa (1994), Houston (1994) and Chicago (1996). In Asia, in Tokyo (1987), Singapore (1988), Hong Kong (two outlets; first opened 1988), Osaka (two outlets; first opened 1988), Bangkok (1992), Fukuoka (1992), Taipei (1992), Kyoto (1993), Seoul (1993), Kuala Lumpur (1994) and Jakarta (1995). In the Middle East, in Dubai (1993) and Jeddah (1995). In Australia, in Sydney (1996).

By the end of the millennium Bulgari is planning to have at least seventy branches worldwide. This formidable network allows Bulgari to spread its unmistakable style and Italian flair throughout the world, and thus to realise the dreams and aspirations of its predecessors. In

268. *Advertisement,* Tappeto di Gemme, *circa 1965.*

1996, the opening of a second shop in Paris, in Place Vendôme, shrine of international high jewellery, is the crowning of the firm's worldwide success.

Apart from Rome, the most important point of reference within the Bulgari network is unquestionably the New York shop. From its very beginning, Bulgari in Rome has been patronised by American tourists. This sparked the firm's awareness of the increasing importance of the American market. Bulgari began to capitalise on this, initially by supplying the United States through company's agent, William Sheer Inc. Then in 1970 the firm opened a first subsidiary in New York, at the

269. *Views of the shop front in Via dei Condotti as it appears today after the renovations of 1981. Note how the windows have been reduced in size in order to draw attention to the jewels displayed in them.*

270. *Views of the entrance hall and the Silver Gallery (above) at Bulgari in Via dei Condotti, Rome, unaltered since they were first designed and lavishly decorated in the 1930s.*

Pierre Hotel, and in 1989 the prestigious shop at 730 Fifth Avenue, on the corner of 57th Street. This is a strategic position situated at one of the most critical retailing intersections in the world. These striking premises occupy the ground floor and first level of the Crown Building, a 1924 skyscraper designed by the architects Warren & Wetmore. Bulgari entrusted architect Piero Sartogo to develop this site. Sartogo's creation is an extraordinary assemblage of glass and two-hundred and fifty tons of *botticino* and pink Asiago marble. At first sight this might appear a harsh, almost crude display, reminiscent of the monumentality and grandeur of antique Roman architecture. Upon closer examination, though, it turns out to be exquisitely detailed, with a softness that comes as a startling surprise. With its subdued, purposely neutral palette – beige, cream and pink –, rounded details of mouldings and edges, and copious use of cherry wood, the

271. *Shop-front of Bulgari's premises opened at 730 Fifth Avenue, New York in 1989. The façade is characterised by a monumental assemblage of* botticino *and pink Asiago marble. Since the 1970s such materials have been chosen by Bulgari to decorate the façades of most of the firm's shops worldwide.*

272. *The façades of the Tokyo and Jeddah Bulgari flagship shops, opened in 1987 and 1995 respectively. These are striking and monumental examples of how Bulgari continues to use the same materials for the decoration of its shops in order to create a unified and recognisable backdrop for its jewels worldwide.*

BVLGARI'S IMAGE

interior design matches in excellence that of Bulgari artefacts, to the extent that crafted object and crafted shop have become one. This is not to suggest, however, that the shop competes with the jewels; on the contrary, it provides an ideal background. Gianni Bulgari stated (*L'Officiel*, May 1980): "We wish to sell our jewels in shops which are the image of what we are and what we do."

The decor and architecture of the flagship shop at 10 Via dei Condotti has also undergone several changes over the years to keep up with the development of Bulgari's aesthetic criteria. When business picked up after the war, the shop was enlarged to include two new rooms and a long gallery for the display of jade carvings and objects. In 1964 part of the first floor was added to the premises. Alterations by architect Piero Sartogo in 1971 gave the shop its present appearance.

Over the years Bulgari has applied similar aesthetic concepts to the design and decor of all its premises throughout the world, though always respecting the local architectural and cultural heritage. This provides a uniform background to complement the beauty of its jewels and reinforces the universality of the Bulgari image.

From Paris to Miami, from Jeddah to Tokyo, from St Moritz to Hong Kong, a homogeneous selection of fine jewellery, objects and watches are presented in settings of consistent decor.

273. *Entrance to the shop in Avenue Montaigne, Paris, opened in 1979.*

274. *Eight façades of Bulgari shops worldwide. These illustrate how Bulgari has applied similar aesthetic concepts to the design of all its shops through respecting the local architectural and cultural heritage.*

Advertising

During the 1960s Bulgari began consolidating its ever-growing international reputation. As a direct consequence, the firm also began developing strong and recognisable advertising images. Therefore it is not surprising that from this time on, one is also able to trace Bulgari's development by viewing the evolution of the firm's advertising campaigns.

At the beginning of the 1960s, the first images to be employed were famous Roman sights used as backdrops for the firm's jewels. Perhaps the most successful of such images is that of a fine ruby and diamond cluster necklace superimposed on a view of the Spanish Steps (ill. 191). This is one of the most famous sights in Rome and is situated at one end of Via dei Condotti, very close to the Bulgari shop. In this instance the message is clear: Bulgari was promoting its exclusive high jewellery – a necklace set with the finest gems – for which the firm was especially renowned at that time.

The view of the Spanish Steps, moreover, reinforces the notion of Rome as Bulgari's one and only outlet. Other images were constructed according to similar criteria. These include famous sights such as the Capitoline Square, designed by Michelangelo, and the keyhole of the Orange Garden on the Aventine Hill, with view of St. Peter's,

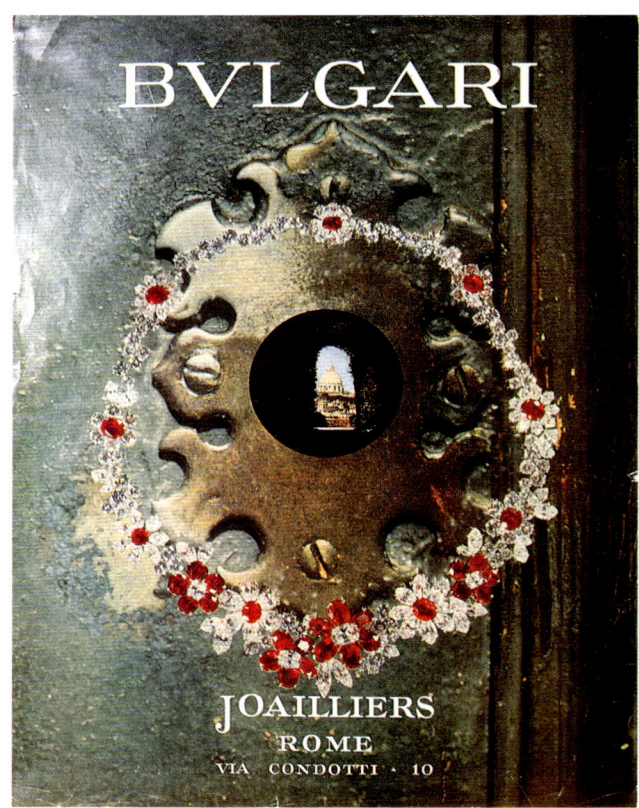

275. *Two images from Bulgari's advertising campaign of the early 1960s, where the firm's fine jewels are superimposed on views of Rome.*

276. *An image from Bulgari's advertising campaign of the mid-1960s. A lion-mask bracelet, set with cabochon rubies and sapphires, and diamonds, is photographed against the background of an antique Chinese jade carving. At this time Bulgari was renowned for selling, besides jewellery and silver, also fine Oriental jades.*

respectively superimposed with a diamond cluster necklace and a ruby and diamond flower necklace.

In all such images the "BVLGARI" logo is formed by white lettering which serves as a title to the page, while the word *Joaillers* – jewellers – in French rather than Italian indicates that the firm was consciously placing itself in the French tradition of jewellery making. This is not surprising as, at the time, Bulgari was still rooted in the French tradition of jewellery design, characterised by motifs of naturalistic inspiration and emphasis on the preciousness of the gems.

In the mid-1960s, the firm began forging a more personal image and style of advertisement. This reflected the development of a more distinctive Bulgari jewellery style, characterised by vibrant colour combinations coupled with the use of cabochon gems. The sights of Rome were abandoned and replaced by backdrops composed of objects and works of art closely associated with the firm.

Among the most striking images of these years is that of a necklace, set with amethysts, emeralds, diamonds and turquoises, lying on a hoard of ancient Roman coins (ill. 56). Equally effective is that of a double lion-mask bracelet set with diamonds, cabochon rubies and sapphires photographed on a carved jade plaque. The choice of ancient silver coins as a background can be explained by the fact that it was about

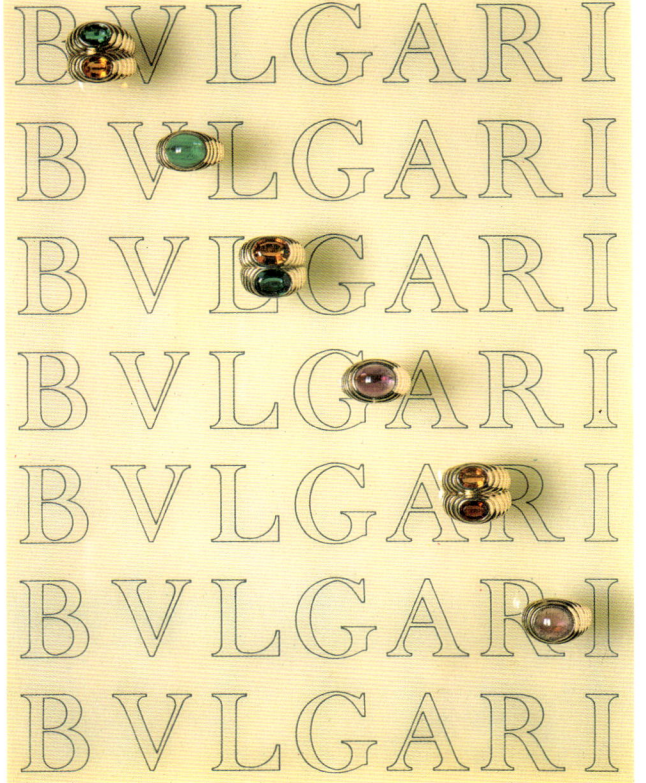

277. *Two images of Bulgari's advertising campaign of the 1970s where the background to the jewels is the repeated logo. From the late 1960s on, the Bulgari style was taking shape and the firm realised the importance of associating it with a recognisable logo.*

this time that Bulgari began mounting ancient coins on its modern jewels. This particular use of coins soon became a Bulgari trademark. Similarly, at this time, fine jade carvings were avidly collected by Bulgari and prominently displayed in the *Galleria delle Giade*, the heart of the Via dei Condotti shop. It is clear therefore that the images of both backgrounds and jewels in these advertisements are especially representative of the firm's activities in the mid-1960s.

Another particularly striking and successful image of these years, known at Bulgari as the *Tappeto di Gemme* (Carpet of Gemstones) consists of a hoard of brooches characteristically set with gems of vibrant colours. In this instance Bulgari's gem-set creations are used successfully both as backdrop and as centrepiece of the image. Only a small gold cartouche inscribed "BVLGARI ROMA" can be clearly identified at the centre (ill. 268).

From the late 1960s on, as the Bulgari style took shape in an increasingly individual and recognisable manner, the importance of associating it with a recognisable logo was not underestimated. In the advertising campaigns of the 1970s, jewels and the "BVLGARI" logo, which had crowned the shop-front in Via dei Condotti since 1934, were given nearly equal importance.

The logo was no longer confined to the title of an advertisement or placed in discrete cartouches at the bottom of an image, but featured prominently as if competing with the jewels themselves.

Throughout the 1970s, the "BVLGARI" logo is employed in a nearly infinite variety of backdrops to the firm's jewels. Initially one finds the inscription "BVLGARI" in large gold lettering, studded with gem-encrusted jewels (ill. 1). This image is then replaced by the repeated logo "BVLGARI BVLGARI", in small scale, rendered in embossed white paper. This was then followed by the same logo embossed in much larger characters, at times on dark, and at times on white paper or even rendered in line drawing.

From the end of the 1970s, the white paper embossed with the "BVLGARI" logo was no longer placed on a flat surface but arranged on a stage-like construction. This was formed by a sloping plane completed by a vertical backdrop, as illustrated in the advertisement depicting a gold and coral *Parentesi* necklace. In this instance, the recognisable Bulgari modular jewellery is reinforced by the nearly obsessive repetition of the firm's logo. The resulting association creates a very powerful image, which is unmistakably Bulgari (ill. 162).

It is its understanding of the strength of the logo which led Bulgari to utilise it above all other images. While the image of the logo reinforces the Bulgari product, other objects might compete and detract from it. This explains why the firm, over the years, has seldom used images such as flowers or female figures in its advertisements. On one occasion, a Bulgari gem-set flower brooch was photographed for an advertisement besides an orange marguerite. When Paolo Bulgari saw it, he exclaimed "God has won!" To his eyes the natural flower seemed more beautiful than the jewelled Bulgari counterpart: he believed that nature is too perfect to off-set something made by man.

278. *Two images of Bulgari's Dream advertising campaign, which spanned from 1980 to 1989. The long-lasting success of these powerful images was due to the surreal association of sky, jewels and Bulgari logo.*

In 1980 a new campaign was introduced: the *Bulgari Dream*. This time Bulgari jewels and objects were placed on sloping stages decorated with the embossed logo. Blue skies scattered with white clouds acted as backdrops. The jewels were actors performing in a fictitious setting. It was a dream-like setting – hence the name of the campaign – characterised by a powerful yet surreal association between sky, jewel and "BVLGARI" logo. It was not coincidental that the inspiration for this artificial construction of space derived from the work of the surrealist artist René Magritte, known for his startling juxtapositions of the ordinary and the strange. In the *Dream* campaign the jewels are never accompanied by a caption; it is their inherent beauty alone which captivates the viewer.

At times one finds a dark menacing sky in conjunction with a steel BVLGARI-BVLGARI wristwatch, at other times one finds a bright dawn-like sky in association with a necklace set with multicoloured sapphires. This surreal juxtaposition of jewel and sky served to convey the message that Bulgari ornaments were suitable for all occasions and wearable at all times: during or after a storm and even in broad daylight. Wearability of a jewel was in fact one of the firm's main concerns from the 1970s on and it is not surprising that it was also reinforced in visual terms. The success of these powerful

BVLGARI'S IMAGE

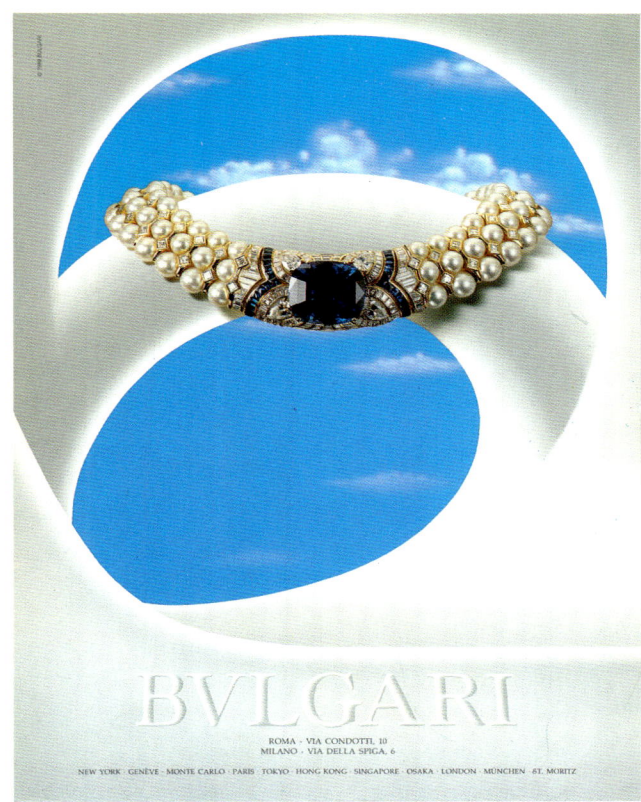

279. *Two images of Bulgari's* Feminine Dream *advertising campaign of 1989-91. By this time the repetition of the logo is abandoned and replaced by a single inscription, "BVLGARI". The jewels are displayed on curved abstract shapes reminiscent of Henry Moore's sculptures, against skies scattered with clouds.*

juxtapositions was such that the criteria of the *Dream* campaign remained unaltered for nearly a decade.

From 1989 until 1991, the dream theme was taken one step further with the *Feminine Dream* campaign. By this time, the repetition of the logo had been completely abandoned and replaced by a single inscription used as a form of base. The jewel was placed on a grey white curving abstract shape inspired by Henry Moore's sculptures, with a background of blue skies scattered with clouds. The shift in emphasis away from the logo had become possible, as recognition was no longer an issue. The firm, however, continued to address its other main concern: the idea that a jewel is something to be worn and enjoyed at all times. By associating bright daylight with jewellery, Bulgari emphasised the concept that a jewel does not have to be worn only in the evening for formal occasions, but, on the contrary, is something to be enjoyed and worn all the times, especially during the day. Furthermore, the bright blues and whites found in *Feminine Dream* evoke the colours of the Mediterranean world and are a reference to the cultural origins of Bulgari.

In 1992, Bulgari launched a new advertising campaign, *Metamorphosis*. The aim was to emphasise the creativity of their jewels and watches and to reinforce the trend for less formal use of jewellery.

280. *In 1992 Bulgari launched a new advertising campaign:* Metamorphosis. *This relies on the depiction of jewels and watches in improper settings where, for example, brooches become windmills, and watches become padlocks on iron gates. Such images reinforce in a novel and memorable manner the concept of "wearability" of a jewel – a concern at Bulgari since the 1970s.*

The pastel-coloured backgrounds, painted in watercolour by artist Davide Pizzigoni, depict fairy tale worlds, at times with ships, hot air balloons, building façades and oil ducts. In this context the jewel serves an improper function, hence the name *Metamorphosis*: necklaces become bridges or anchor chains for ships, rings fasten the sail of a boat or serve as door knockers, and watches or bracelets substitute gauges or padlocks on iron gates. Surprisingly, in this context, the substitution of a non-precious object with a jewel paradoxically renders the seemingly superfluous jewel indispensable. This image therefore reinforces, in a novel and striking manner, the concept of wearability, at the heart of Bulgari's philosophy. Speaking of the new campaign, Paolo Bulgari said: "We wanted a type of communication never implemented before in the jewellery world, which would underline the passion we dedicate in designing and producing our jewels and watches, and which would not be afraid of playing them down." Since the 1960s the common denominator of all Bulgari advertising is its originality and often daring qualities which visually capture the firm's different concerns over time. The jewels are nearly always left to speak for themselves, unaided by flowery captions. Ultimately, it is their pure beauty which attracts the viewer.

Bibliography

Balfour, I., *Famous Diamonds*, London 1987

Bernareggi, E., *Istituzioni di Numismatica Antica*, Terza Edizione, Milano 1992

Burnett, A., *Coins*, London 1991

Clerici, A., *Disegni per Gioielli della Ditta Bulgari negli Anni Venti*, Tesi di Laurea, Milano, 1987-1988

Dalloro, G., *Minted by Bulgari*, in: *FMR* no. 38

Dalloro, G., *Bulgari, Gemme nummarie,* in: *FMR* no. 71, Milano 1989

D'Annunzio, G., *Il Piacere*, 1889

Desyllas, N., Milionis, C., *Epirus, An Aesthetic Wonder Throughout a Greek Region*, Athens 1994

Dubbs Ball, J., *Jewellery of the Stars*, West Chester 1991

Gabardi, M., *Gioielli Anni Cinquanta*, Milano 1986

Goldberger, B., *730 Fifth Avenue*, Milano 1990

Gregorietti, G., *Il Gioiello nei Secoli*, Milano 1969

Kita, T., *Kekkai*, Milan, 1991

Lenti, L., *Gioielli e Gioiellieri di Valenza*, Torino 1994

Newton, C.M., *A Barrel of Diamonds*, New York 1980

Proddow, P., Healy, D., Fasel, M., *Hollywood Jewels*, New York 1992

Proddow, P., Healy, D., *American Jewellery, Glamour and Tradition*, New York 1987

Raulet, S., *Bijoux des Années 1940-1950*, Paris 1987

Rutter, S., *Greek Coinage*, Aylesbury 1983

Schlumberger, E., *Un présent pour le souverain pontife et d'autre joyaux des XVI et XVII siècles vus chez un grand antiquaire de Rome*, in: *Connaissance des Arts*, December 1963

Snowman, K. et alii, *The Master Jewelers*, London 1990

Zeri, F., *Confesso che ho sbagliato. Ricordi autobiografici*, Milano 1995

SALE ROOM CATALOGUES

Elton John Jewellery, Sotheby's London, September 1988

Elton John Jewellery, Sotheby's London, December 1993

Jewellery and Silver by Bulgari, Christie's St Moritz, February 1993

The Andy Warhol Collection, Jewellery and Watches, Sotheby's New York, December 1988

The Jewels and Objects of Vertu of the Honorable Clare Boothe Luce, Sotheby's New York, April 1988

London, Geneva and New York sale room jewellery catalogues published between 1990 and 1995 were also thoroughly researched.

EXHIBITION CATALOGUES

Moscati S. et alii, *I Celti*, Milano 1991

Acknowledgements

Our first thanks go to Paolo and Nicola Bulgari, and to all those at Bulgari worldwide who helped us to obtain and collate the numerous tesserae of this elaborate and exciting mosaic. We are particularly grateful to Catherine Robert for her invaluable help in gathering material and information.

We also would like to thank the following colleagues, friends and collectors for their advice, suggestions, information and photographic material they have so generously provided:

Theodore Allegaert, New York
Farida Al Zamil, London
Giovanni Antonelli, Milan
Brunella and Gaio Bacci, Rome
Victor Franco de Baux, Sotheby's London
Guiduccio Bedarid, Paris
Bernard Berger, Sotheby's Geneva
Paula Billingsley, Milan
René H. Bittel, Bozell Advertising SA, Geneva
Gianni Bulgari, Rome
Anna Bulgari Calissoni, Roma
Marina Bulgari Spaccarelli, Marina B, Geneva
Robert Casson, London
Harry Charteris, Sotheby's London
Anne Choate, Christie's Geneva
Maddalena Costa, Christie's New York
Marina Crescenzi Foggi, Crescenzi, Rome
Nunzi Crescenzi Sperati, Crescenzi, Rome
Pier Vittorio Crova, Crova, Valenza
Sarah Curran, London
Giorgio De Marchi, Rome
Andrea M. De Reguardati, Zendrini, Rome
Nicole and Jean-Claude Duhem, Duhem, Paris
Tom Eden, Sotheby's London
Carlo Ferrero Zendrini, Rome
Angela Folino, Christie's New York
Giorgio Gasparetto, Crova, Valenza
Mark Gisbourn, Sotheby's Institute, London
Laura Grandi, Milan
Gian Luca Illario, Carlo Illario e Fratelli, Valenza
Nigel Israel, London
Catherine Johns, The British Museum, London
Flaminia Lisi, Rome
Colin Mackay, Sotheby's London
Giuseppe Mascetti, Varese
Federica Mascetti Paggi, Dal Mondo, Varese
Priscilla Medici, Medici, Rome
Bonnie Morris, London
Isabelle de La Moussaye, Sotheby's Geneva
Stefano Papi, Sotheby's Rome
Alexei Sapsford, London
Philip Sapsford, London
Piero Sartogo, Sartogo, Rome
Inez Stodel, Amsterdam
Lia Trapani, Naples
Anthea Triossi, Rome
Luigi Triossi, Rome
Caroline Turrian, Geneva
Daniele Turrian, Sotheby's Geneva
Marina Valli, Rome
Serena Vergano, Bofil, Barcelona
Nathalie Vianello Chiodo, Christie's Geneva
Mimma Viglezio, Hill & Knowlton, Milan
Aldo Vitali, Vitali, Rome
Valerie Vlasaty, Sotheby's New York
Jurg Wille, Sotheby's Zurich

Our special thanks are addressed to all the private collectors who generously allowed their jewels to be illustrated in this book.

Photographic Credits

Alfredo Agomeri, Rome: 35, 38, 39, 40, 41, 42, 43, 44, 45
Joel von Allmen, Neuchâtel: 167, 261
Javier Alvarez / Courtesy *L'Officiel*, June 1983: 54
Angeli Photo News Agency: 51
Archivo Bofill, Barcelona: 161
Archivio Bulgari, Rome: 4, 5, 7, 8, 9, 10, 11, 16, 17, 23, 24, 25, 26, 27, 28, 30, 31, 32, 50, 52, 53, 55, 93, 112, 114, 125, 127, 151, 154, 155, 156, 157, 161, 163, 166, 170, 171, 172, 173, 177, 178, 181, 182, 190, 193, 203, 204, 205 (drawings), 206 (drawing, earrings), 220, 239, 240, 241, 247, 249, 257, 265, 269, 270, 271, 272, 273, 274, 277, 278, 279
Archivio Crescenzi, Rome: 6, 14, 36
Archive Duhem, Paris: 103, 105, 110, 115 (drawing), 117 (drawing), 118, 119, 121, 122
Gaio Bacci, Rome: 1, 56, 98, 111, 113, 117 (jewel), 120, 128, 129, 130, 131, 132, 133, 149, 150, 162, 164, 165, 174, 175, 176, 180, 191, 205 (drawing), 212, 216, 232, 245, 250, 251, 263, 268, 275 (right)
Aldo Ballo, Milan: 200
René H. Bittel, Bozell Advertising, Geneva: 232, 276, 280
Robert Emmett Bright, Rome: 275 (left)
The British Museum, London, 143, 144, 145
Ray Buonanno, New York: 107 (on page 86), 109, 153, 186, 225, 228, 229
Umberto Buzzacchi, Rome: 13, 18, 19, 21, 22, 62, 94, 95, 158, 160, 234, 235, 236, 237, 240
Christie's: 68 (on page 57), 69 (bracelet), 80, 85, 88, 89, 92, 104, 108 (front views), 115 (jewel), 152, 194, 233
Michel Comte / Courtesy *Vogue* Italia: 47, 48
N. Desyllas, *Epirus. An Aesthetic Wander Through a Greek Region*, Synolo Publications, Athens: 3
Terence Donovan, London: 33
Claudio Elia, Rome: 238, 239, 240
Claudio Elia / Courtesy *Argento!*, March 1991: 241, 242
Carlo Facchini, Milan: 243, 254, 256, 260, 267
Piero Gemelli, Milan: 264
Marian Gérard, Geneva: 68 (on page 56), 71
Iran Issa-Khan / Courtesy *Harper's Bazaar*, May 1983: 54
Istituto dell'Enciclopedia Italiana, Rome: 12
Bill King / Courtesy *Vanity Fair*, November 1984: 54
Bill King / Courtesy *Vogue* Paris, April 1982: 54

Design Richard Bernstein, photo Barry McKinley / Courtesy *Interview*, Brant Publications, Inc., April 1979: 54
Alberto Lavit / Courtesy Dal Mondo Collection, Varese: 2
Photo L&I, New York: 52
Paul Lange / Courtesy *Vogue* Deutsch, November 1991: 54
Courtesy Microsoft: 49
Daniel Mille, Montecarlo: 96, 97
Michael Oldford, New York: 159
Oriani & Origone, Milan: 266
Claudio Paggiarino, Milan: 253, 255, 259
Studio Panoulis, Athens: 53
Norman Parkinson / Courtesy *Town & Country*, June 1989: 54
François Peyrou, Photo Reflets, Geneva: 82, 106, 124, 183, 184, 196, 197, 198, 199, 201, 202, 205 (jewels), 244
John Quinn, London: 86, 248
Ranzini, Milan: 258
Alex Rossellini / Courtesy *Amica*, 25 February 1991 / Grazia Neri: 207
Sipa Press / Courtesy *Votre Beauté*, February 1995: 37
J. Frederick Smith / Courtesy *Town & Country*, September 1990: 54
Sotheby's: 35, 76, 79, 81, 90, 107 (on page 87), 116, 117 (drawing), 123, 146, 147, 159, 192, 195, 206 (bracelet)
Saskia van Stegeren, Rome: 20, 29, 57, 58, 59, 60, 61, 63, 64, 65, 66, 67, 70, 72, 73, 74, 75, 77, 78, 83, 84, 87, 91, 99, 100, 101, 102, 108 (reverse), 134, 135, 136, 137, 138, 139, 140, 141, 142, 148, 168, 169, 179, 185, 187, 188, 189, 208, 209, 210, 211, 213, 214, 215, 217, 218, 219, 221, 222, 223, 224, 226, 227, 230, 231, 246, 252
Felix Streuli, Zurich: 262
Tyen, Paris: 126
Photo Valesko / *Los Angeles Daily News* / Saga - Grazia Neri: 46
Vasari, Rome: 15

The information contained in this volume has been furnished by various sources and carefully examined. The publishers apologise for any errors or omissions.

Daniela Mascetti F.G.A., Director of Sotheby's Jewellery Department, London, graduated at Milan Statale University in Classics and specialised in Archaeology. Since 1980 she began working for Sotheby's. In 1982 she graduated in Gemmology in Great Britain. She regularly lectures on the history of jewellery and has published *Gioielli dell'800* (1984), *Oreficeria del '700* (1985), *Understanding Jewellery* (1989) co-author David Bennett, *Earrings* (1990) co-author Amanda Triossi.

Amanda Triossi F.G.A., Consultant of Sotheby's Jewellery Department, Associate Lecturer of Sotheby's Institute, London. Graduated in History of Art at Cambridge University. From 1986 she has been associated with Sotheby's. In 1988 she graduated in Gemmology in Great Britain. She set up and runs since 1992 the *Understanding Jewellery Course* in London. She has lectured and holds regular seminars on the history of jewellery design for Sotheby's and other institutions worldwide. She published *Earrings* (1990) co-author Daniela Mascetti.

Rev 9/22

EAST BATON ROUGE PARISH LIBRARY
BATON ROUGE, LOUISIANA

MAIN

DISCARD